TRUE PRINCESS

by Erin Davis

LifeWay Press®
Nashville, TN

ISBN: 978-1-4158-6842-3
Item Number: 005260396

Dewey Decimal Classification Number: 248.83
Subject Heading:
CHRISTIAN LIFE \ HUMILITY \ RESPONSIBILITY

Printed in the United States of America

Student Ministry Publishing
LifeWay Resources
One LifeWay Plaza
Nashville, TN 37234

We believe that the Bible has God for its author; salvation for its end;
and truth, without any mixture of error, for its matter and that all
Scripture is totally true and trustworthy. The 2000 statement of
The Baptist Faith and Message is our doctrinal guideline.

Table of Contents

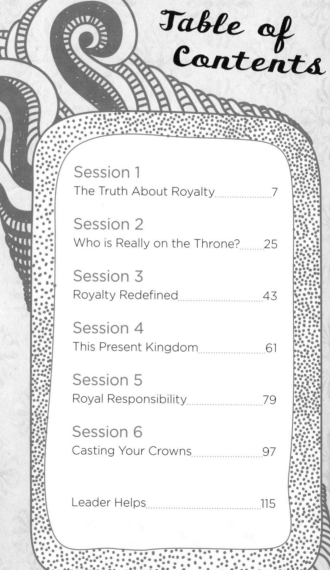

About the author

ERIN DAVIS is a popular author, blogger, and speaker who loves to see women of all ages run to the deep well of God's Word. She is the author of many resources for young women including *Graffiti, Beautiful Encounters*, and the *My Name Is Erin* series. She also co-authored the companion guide for *Lies Young Women Believe*. When she's not writing, you can find Erin chasing chickens and children on her small farm in the Midwest.

Jason and Erin live in Southwest Missouri. Erin's quest for the perfect scoop of ice cream is never-ending and her sons—Eli, Noble, and Judah—are her constant source of entertainment.

Special thanks

The young women I've encountered through student ministry laid the foundation for this resource. My conversations with you over endless slices of pizza or sips of caramel lattes helped me understand what needed to be written and drove me deeper and deeper into God's Word for answers. You constantly challenge me to live out what I teach and to ditch the diva in myself. I love teaching you and watching God work in your lives. It is my great pleasure to discover God's Truth alongside you. Thank you for letting me walk beside you.

For leaders: How to use this study

Weekly study

If you will be using this resource as a weekly Bible study for girls, you will probably want to teach the book over six weeks. For large group time, use the First Glance section of each session. Additional teaching plans can be found on pages 115-128. The girls will complete three days of individual study between group meetings. These individual study sections are titled Second Look.

Event-based study

If you intend to use this study for an event (like a retreat or lock-in), complete the number of First Glance sessions based upon how many sessions of group Bible study times you'll have that weekend. (Most DiscipleNow models include five teaching times.) Using this model, you will teach the First Glance sections to a large group and allow time for girls to work through the individual lessons (Second Look, parts 1, 2, and 3) during quiet times or in small groups (or a combination of the two).

Individual study

Every session includes three individual study segments. In order to get the most out of this study, the girls in your group really need to complete their "homework" outside of the large group teaching time. Let them know from the start of this study that the individual sessions aren't optional. If you offer up the challenge, many girls will be willing to complete the homework.

Make a point to regularly encourage them to do the individual study. Here are some creative ways to spur them on:

1. **Start a Facebook group for your study.** Regularly post thoughts, ideas, and questions on the group's wall. Use it as a forum to remind them to do their individual study.
2. **Send out reminder postcards.** Getting regular mail is a treasure in today's electronic world!
3. **Set up accountability partners** in the first session. Have the girls hold each other accountable to do the individual work.

Weekly activities

At the end of each session, you can incorporate the following activities.

Alone time

You will wrap up your group study each week by giving the girls some alone time. Tell them that this time is designed to help them process what they've learned and to let God speak to them about any changes He'd like to make in their lives. The tone of the room should be quiet and reflective.

Journal

If you decide to incorporate journaling into your large group study time, give each girl a journal. Conclude each session by asking the girls to journal about what they've learned and what God is teaching them. Tell them they can use their journals to write letters to God, draw, create poetry, write songs, or record their thoughts.

Prayer prompts

Each week you will place index cards throughout the room with specific prayer prompts written on them. Encourage girls to move silently from card to card using each prompt as a way to begin a conversation with God. If they'd like, they can record their thoughts and prayers in their journals. Use the list of prayer prompts below and/or supplement them with your own.

Week 1:
- Lord, one thing I want to learn through this study is...
- I know you want to change my heart in the area of...
- God, thank you for adopting me into your family. It means so much because...
- One area of my life where I haven't honored you is...
- Lord, teach me how to minister to the other girls in this group. (Stop and pray for each girl by name.)

Week 2:
- Jesus, when I hear about the kind of King You are, I feel...
- Lord, it is hard to shift my focus away from myself because...
- Jesus, one area where I haven't made You King is...
- God, I want to worship You more because...
- Heavenly Father, one thing You are teaching me right now is...

Week 3:
- Jesus, when I think about Your humble birth, I feel...
- I am so thankful that You came to earth to deliver the message that...
- Jesus, it is hard for me to grasp that You chose to take on human flesh because...
- I am so thankful for Your gift of salvation because...

Week 4:
- Lord, sometimes the treasures of this world seem so alluring, especially...
- God, help me to pursue treasures that last...
- Lord, I am learning that Your kingdom is more important than...
- God, when I think about the treasures in Your kingdom, I feel...

Week 5:
- Father, I am thankful that You saved me from my sin because...
- Lord, one area of my life where I need You to make me new is...
- God, thank You for teaching me that my inheritance from You is...
- Father, teach me the areas of my life I need to work on in order to live more like a daughter of the King.

THE TRUTH ABOUT ROYALTY

First Glance

The tables are set with white linen and fine china. Seated at each table are groups of girls whispering excitedly as they nibble tiny sandwiches and yummy desserts. Some girls are sipping hot tea from fine china teacups. Everyone in the room is wearing a tiara. Adults circle the room giving out kind words of affirmation. One message is repeated over and over throughout the evening: "You are a princess."

The scene I'm describing wasn't ripped from the pages of a high society magazine. This isn't a royal banquet taking place inside a castle (although it was designed to feel like it). In fact, this scene can be found most often in church youth rooms and fellowship halls. The girls made to feel like princesses are *you*.

In case you haven't noticed, there's been a movement to convince young women like you that you're all princesses. "Pure Princess" retreats and "daughter of the King" banquets are planned at churches just like yours in an attempt to show you your value as a child of God.

But where *exactly* does this idea that we are princesses come from? What *exactly* does it mean to be a daughter of the King?

GROUP ACTIVITY
Surely this princess concept comes from God's Word, right? Find out! Get into pairs and do a quick search using a Bible concordance or online Bible search engine. Find the specific passages where Scripture talks about being a princess. List them in the space provided below. Ready, set, search!

Defining a princess

All of us have an image in our minds of what a princess should be like. Circle the words below that match your perception of princesses.

Crowned	Beautiful	Servant	Fairy Tale
Dramatic	Meek	Entitled	Diva
Adored	Selfish	Responsible	Meek
Submissive	Well-dressed	High-Maintenance	

Let's take it one step further. Use the statements below to define your concept of what it means to be a princess.

■ A princess looks like...

■ A princess acts like...

Most of us have a similar vision of a princess. She's beautiful. She's decked out in a gorgeous gown and a sparkling crown. She's also spoiled and is a bit of a diva. In many ways, her life is easier than most. There's no shortage of people waiting to satisfy her needs and wants.

This version of royalty is easy to find. She's in every Disney movie we've ever watched. She is the stuff that fairy tales are made of.

But is this the kind of princess that God designed *us* to be? Does our definition of princess match up with the way we are described in God's Word?

Proving your royal heritage

As you already discovered from your Bible search, there is no passage that says, "Thou art princesses." But that doesn't mean that this concept of royalty can't be found in Scripture.

Beside the following passages, write out the portion of Scripture that mentions royalty.

■ 1 Timothy 6:15-16

■ Revelation 19:16

■ Romans 8:15-17

■ Ephesians 1:4-5

■ **God is the .... He has adopted me as his .... That makes me a ....!**

Because you are the adopted daughter of the King of kings, you are indeed a princess. But more importantly, you are the daughter of the King. Take a moment to write a note of thanks to God for adopting you.

Jesus, thank you for adopting me into your family. Knowing this truth makes me feel special because...

PICTURE OF A PRINCESS Draw your idea of the perfect princess in the space provided below. Don't worry; you won't be graded on artistic talent. Focus your artwork on expressing your perception of how a princess looks, acts, and lives.

9

A NEW
PICTURE

A NEW PICTURE

I hope you didn't put away those art supplies too soon! Pull them back out and create a new image of a princess. This time, focus on what it looks like to be a daughter of the King. How does this change a princess' appearance and behavior? In order to make the distinction even more clear, after you've finished drawing, add some descriptive words to your picture.

Princess vs. daughter of the King

I'd like you to shift your focus from seeing yourself as a princess to seeing yourself as the daughter of the King. That may seem like a silly distinction, but trust me, there's a huge difference between *acting* like a princess and *being* the daughter of a king (especially the King of kings).

■ What is the princess' responsibility to her father, the king?

■ How is a princess expected to treat her father?

■ In what ways does a princess represent her father?

■ How should a princess respond to her father's decisions?

Hollywood may lead us to believe that princesses can do what they want whenever they want with no accountability or authority in their lives. But this simply isn't the case. Being a princess comes with great responsibility. You aren't called to act like a spoiled brat. You are called to honor the King.

Write out Psalm 45:11 in the margin. Circle the portions of the passage that describe how God, the King, feels about you. Underline the portions of the passage that describe how you should respond.

■ In your own words, define the word "honor."

■ What does it mean to honor the King?

■ What are three specific ways you can honor God today?

Making the distinction

Are you beginning to see the difference between *acting* like a princess and *living* like a daughter of the King? You'll be digging even deeper into these truths during your personal study throughout the week. For now, think about the differences between the world's portrayal of a princess and God's calling to live as a daughter of the King.

Being a princess	Being a daughter of the King

Which kind of princess are you?

Quiz

Are you living like a princess or a daughter of the King? Answer true or false to the following questions to find out.

T or F   I love being the center of attention.

T or F   When making a decision, I don't usually consider the truth in God's Word.

T or F   My friends think I'm a drama queen.

T or F   It's hard for me to find time to help others.

T or F   I feel like I deserve certain things.

T or F   Love doesn't require sacrifice.

T or F   The way I spend my time and money is my business.

T or F   I want to be taken care of.

T or F   The things I watch and listen to have nothing to do with my relationship with God.

T or F   I couldn't live without my cell phone, iPod®, or computer.

Mostly true—Princess alert! There's a part of you that wants to be like the princesses you see in movies and fairy tales. You like to be comfortable and avoid making sacrifices and serving others. You're drawn to the things that culture promises will bring fulfillment. If you're in this category, don't worry. You'll be doing some deep digging into God's Word over the next few sessions. The promises God offers you can motivate you to live out *His* plan for your life. We'll look at lots of practical ways you can make changes in order to live more like a daughter of the King of kings.

Mostly false—Living like a daughter of the King! No divas here. You're already living out some of the qualities of a daughter of the King. But that doesn't mean you can tune out for the rest of this study. There's still plenty of work to be done in your heart and life.

PART 1: What's in a name?

The pop princesses of our culture have a reputation for rebellion. It's no surprise when their scandals hit the headlines and their behavior is photographed for the world to see. These "princesses" don't seem to worry about honoring their family name or protecting the reputation of their fathers.

We may call these girls princesses, but deep down we know this isn't how a princess should act. These aren't the kind of young women we should admire. Their lives aren't the stuff of fairy tales.

A princess is special because she is the daughter of someone special. Everything she does points toward her father, the king. If a princess acts recklessly or ignores the needs or customs of her people, it isn't just *her* reputation that suffers. *The honor and image of the throne is at stake.*

Honoring the family name may seem like an ancient concept to our modern brains. But it is a key responsibility of a daughter of our King, and it's a theme repeated often in Scripture.

The following Scriptures will give you some insight into the importance of an honorable reputation. Beside each passage, write down the value of a good name.

■ Proverbs 3:3-4

■ Proverbs 22:1

■ Ecclesiastes 7:1a

As God's adopted daughters, we have a responsibility to honor God and reflect His character. We need to honor His reputation. This is the mark of a true princess.

Take a moment to reflect on how you can use the following areas of your life to honor your King. Write one specific action you can take in each area.

■ The way I use my time

■ The plans I make for my future

■ The way I act online

■ The way I dress

■ The way I treat others

Mixed messages

As Christians, everything we do sends a message to others. Scripture puts it this way:

> "Therefore, whether you eat or drink, or *whatever you do, do everything for God's glory.*" (1 Cor. 10:31, emphasis added).

Everything we do either brings glory or dishonor to God. In other words, we are Christ's ambassadors. We have a responsibility to represent the King.
    The idea that we are Christ's ambassadors is clear in Scripture.

Read the following passages below. Answer the questions listed with each.

2 Corinthians 5:18-21   Ephesians 6:19-20

ACTIVITY: In your own words, write a definition for the word "ambassador."

Whom are you representing?		
What are your responsibilities as Christ's ambassador?		
What's the King done for you that you can tell others?		

Part 2: Living by the rules of the kingdom

By the law of the kingdom, Princess Jasmine was forced to marry a prince. Princess Ariel was scolded by the king for spending her days at the ocean's surface instead of in royal choir rehearsals. Cinderella had to wait for an invitation to a royal ball before she could have a shot at happily ever after.

These are the princesses we know best. But even their lives weren't all about tiaras, ball gowns, and princes. Their choices were often dictated by others. They submitted to the laws of the kingdom.

While royalty certainly has its perks, it isn't the carefree life we often imagine it to be. True princesses live in discipline and submission.

Do words like "discipline" and "submission" make you want to reconsider your royal role? Does your idea of a disciplined life line up with the standards presented in God's Word? Take the quiz below to find out.

 Does discipline make you cringe?

■ Rules are:
   a) meant to be broken
   b) for my own protection
   c) a major bummer

■ A synonym for *discipline* is:
   a) punishment
   b) instruction
   c) improvement

■ When your parents enforce rules, you usually respond by:
   a) rolling your eyes
   b) expressing your opinion, then doing what they ask
   c) it depends on the rule

■ When it comes to the subject of discipline, God's Word:
   a) has some great advice
   b) is pretty confusing
   c) seems too old fashioned

- God disciplines His children because:
  a) He loves us
  b) He is a just God
  c) He's not really good

- Rebellion seems...
  a) glamorous
  b) dangerous
  c) a normal part of being a teenager

How did you do? This quiz doesn't have an answer key because it was designed to help you start thinking about your attitude toward discipline and submission to others. A disciplined life isn't easy. There are times when submitting to the rules and expectations of others is downright frustrating. But there are benefits of submitting to the rules of God's kingdom.

To whom do you belong?

As daughters of the King, our lives are not our own. Scripture says:

> *Or didn't you realize that your body is a sacred place, the place of the Holy Spirit? Don't you see that you can't live however you please, squandering what God paid such a high price for? —1 Corinthians 6:19a, The Message*

Being adopted into God's family means allowing Him to be in charge. He sits on the throne of your heart, and your choices should be determined by His will. It is critical for you to realize that your life is under the authority of the King. You are called to live a life in submission to Christ.

You are probably living out this principle in some areas of your life. Write out how becoming a Christian has changed the following:

- The way I spend my time

- The way I treat others

- The people with whom I spend my time

Knowing the rules of the Kingdom

Being a daughter of the King should also change the standards by which we live. Princesses must know and live by the rules of their family's kingdom. God has given us the laws of His kingdom through His Word. But this is no ordinary set of laws.

Write out the following Scriptures in your own words. Pay close attention to how God's Word can specifically impact your life.

■ Psalm 18:30 ....

....

■ Psalm 19:7 ....

....

■ Psalm 119:43 ....

....

■ Hebrews 4:12 ....

....

God's Word is living and active. His laws are perfect. The rules of His kingdom are trustworthy. We can put our hope in them. Submission to the rules of God's kingdom is in our best interest. But in order to *follow* God's rules, we must *know* them—which brings us to the concept of discipline.

Knowing the Word: A royal discipline

Sometimes the laws of the land can be downright silly. Check out the list of laws below. Circle the ones that you think are actually on the books in the United States.

■ In Alabama, it is illegal to wear a fake moustache that causes laughter in church.

■ Flirtation between members of the opposite sex on the streets of Little Rock, Arkansas, may result in a 30-day jail term.

■ Chicago law prohibits eating in a place that is on fire.

■ No one may catch fish with his bare hands in Kansas.

■ It is illegal in Michigan to hitch a crocodile to a fire hydrant.[1]

Believe it or not, all of these are actual laws. Besides being silly, these laws are nearly impossible to follow because they aren't known by the citizens.

God's laws aren't silly. They are perfect and trustworthy. But we can't live by them if we don't know them. In order to know them, we must regularly study God's Word. The psalmist put it this way; *"I have treasured Your word in my heart so that I may not sin against You"* (Ps. 119:11).

Hiding God's Word in our hearts requires discipline. We can't depend on our parents or youth ministers or pastors to teach us biblical truth. We must study it *ourselves*. For most Christians, regularly studying the Word can seem overwhelming.

Write down the top five obstacles that keep you from regularly studying God's Word. I've listed a few to get you started.

- *"I'm too busy."*
- *"Reading the Bible feels boring to me."*
- *"I don't understand it."*
- ....
- ....
- ....
- ....
-

When you look at them on paper, don't those excuses seem kind of lame? Does it change your perspective to know that God's laws are perfect (Ps. 19:7) and that the Bible is a living book (Heb. 4:12)? The bottom line is this: in order to live as daughters of the King, we *must* read His Word. Here are some tips for how to start spending more time in the Word:

1. **Get an accountability partner.** Find another believer who agrees to ask you regularly if you've been reading your Bible. Make plans to meet with that friend weekly to discuss what God is teaching you through His Word.

2. **Get rid of time snatchers.** Often, we don't read our Bibles because we simply run out of time. What activities or habits are robbing you of the time you need each day to read the Word? Some possibilities might include Facebook, TV, and sleep. How can you change your choices in these areas to allow more time for studying the Bible?

3. **Find a reading plan that motivates you.** You can read through the Bible in a year, do a topical study on a subject that interests you, study certain biblical characters, or study a specific book of the Bible. Don't just flip open your Bible and read the first thing you see. Choose a plan that helps you dig into His Word. Then stick to that plan.

4. **Memorize Scripture.** Memorizing passages of Scripture is a great way to let God's Word marinate in your heart. Make a concentrated effort to memorize Scripture that reminds you of how God calls you to live.

5. **Make a commitment you can keep.** If a behavior is repeated for 30 days, it is more likely to become a habit. Make a commitment to study your Bible every day for the next 30 days. Keep your commitment manageable. Don't set out to read your Bible for an hour every day. Don't try to set any new world records for Bible speed-reading. Set a manageable goal and commit to follow through for the next 30 days.

What would you add to this list? What advice would you give to a friend who is looking for ways to study God's Word more regularly? List three things below.

- ....
- ....
- ....

Go back to the lists above and choose one action you can take today to start spending more time in God's Word. To solidify your commitment, write out your action step below and sign and date it. For added accountability, share your commitment with the other girls in your study the next time you meet together.

I realize that in order to live like a princess, I need to know the rules of the kingdom. I want to understand God's laws better by studying His Word more often. I commit to take the following step toward more consistent studying of God's Word by ....
....

(write your action step in the above blanks).

Signature: ....
Date: ....

Second Look

PART 3: Embracing the adventure God has for you

We're delighted when the princess and her prince ride off into the sunset to enjoy the life of adventure that awaits. We cheer when a princess defeats a dragon or witch or evil king. We love it when she escapes a dungeon or tower against dangerous odds. We love the adventurous life of a princess.

But surely adventure is lost if being a princess is truly about submission, right? Wrong.

Quiz *How adventurous are you?*

- Your best friend talks you into taking a dance class after school. When it comes time for your recital, you:
  - a) invite everyone you know to come watch your sweet moves
  - b) hide in the back row
  - c) fake a broken leg

- A friend calls you and asks you to join her on a hike. You:
  - a) grab your hiking boots and head out the door
  - b) ask her to walk around the school track with you instead
  - c) stay on the couch. You're not a spur-of-the-moment gal.

- Your church mission team is planning a trip to Zambia, Africa. You:
  - a) sign up for the trip and start tent shopping
  - b) sign up but pack an air mattress and a week's worth of food
  - c) sign up for next year's trip to Daytona Beach, Florida

- When it comes to your hair, you think:
  - a) "Change is good!"
  - b) "It's fun to make subtle changes every once in awhile."
  - c) "I'll just stick with what works."

■ On the last youth ski trip, you:
  a) rented a snowboard and headed for the top of the mountain
  b) stuck with your friends on the moderately easy slopes
  c) never left the lodge

■ Your friends describe you as:
  a) crazy and spontaneous
  b) practical and fun
  c) organized and dependable

■ What's your favorite movie genre?
  a) thrillers
  b) drama
  c) chick flicks

So, how adventurous are you? Add up your As, Bs, and Cs.

Mostly As. You're a thrill seeker. You want adventure. You're drawn toward whatever makes your adrenaline pump. You get bored easily.

Mostly Bs. You love adventure but have a practical side. No one would accuse you of being an adrenaline junkie, but you're not likely to be found on the sidelines either. You love to have fun as long as it's relatively safe.

Mostly Cs. You play it safe. You stick to what you know and value routine. You may love to experience adventure vicariously through movies or friends, but you won't be going bungee jumping any time soon.

What's the most adventurous thing you've ever done?

....

....

A God-sized adventure

The idea that living like a true princess means submitting to the will of someone else may make you feel like you'll be throwing your chances for adventure right out the window, but as daughters of the King, that couldn't be further from the truth. Unlike a princess who may or may not like the life that is chosen for her, we are in for the ride of our lives when we embrace what God has in store for us.

Write out the following passages below. Then go back and circle the benefits to us when we trust in God. Underline the gifts He promises us in these passages. Draw a box around words that describe your future.

■ Psalm 37:4-6

....

....

....

....

■ Proverbs 3:5-6

....

....

....

....

■ Jeremiah 29:11

....

....

....

....

■ Romans 12:2

....

....

....

....

Living our lives in submission to Christ doesn't mean abandoning all hopes of adventure. God is able to provide a life for us that is infinitely more exciting and fulfilling than anything we could create for ourselves. He isn't a power-hungry King who will demand that we make choices that will lead to misery. He is our loving Creator. We can trust what He has in store for us.

But there's more...

It isn't just adventure that draws us toward princesses. We're drawn to the idea that their lives matter. Their lives are more spectacular than the average citizen. We want the same to be true for us. We need to know that we matter, that our lives count for something significant. God alone can satisfy that need in us.

Read the passages on the next page and list in the space provided what each tells you about your significance.

■ Jeremiah 31:3 ....
....
....

■ Psalm 45:11 ....
....
....

■ 1 John 3:1 ....
....
....

Now that is the stuff of fairy tales! God describes His love for you as everlasting. Your beauty enthralls Him. The Bible says that He lavishes His love on you so that you can be called His child. If you are looking for evidence that you matter, look no further. God's Word is clear that you are deeply loved by the King of kings.

When God describes His love for me as "everlasting," it means...

When I read that God thinks I'm beautiful, I feel...

Submitting my life to Christ is difficult for me because...

One area I need to submit to God is...

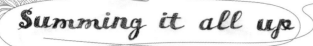

Summing it all up

Here's a quick summary of what you have learned this week.

1. God is the .... **. He** .... **me into His family. That makes me a** ....**!**

Romans 8:15-17 announces our adoption. As daughters of the <u>King</u>, we are <u>adopted</u> into His family as <u>princess</u>es. However, God's kingdom is not the place for a diva mentality. *Have you been acting like a princess instead of seeking to live in a way that honors God? If so, take time now to ask God's forgiveness. Ask Him to teach you what it means to be His daughter.*

2. Everything I do brings glory or dishonor to God. In other words, I am Christ's .... **.**

Read 2 Corinthians 5:20. *Have you been living as if your own reputation is the only thing at stake? Are you most concerned with how your choices impact your own life? In what areas do you need to make changes to better honor Him?* Remember, you are His <u>ambassador</u>.

3. In order to .... **the rules of God's kingdom, I must regularly read His** .... **.**

Part of being a princess is submitting to the laws of God's kingdom. In order to <u>follow</u> God's law, we must know it. In order to know His <u>Word</u>, we must spend time reading, studying, and meditating on it.

Review the steps you committed to take toward reading the Bible more often. What steps are you willing to take this week? ....
....

4. When I submit my life to Christ, I am in for a .... **- sized** .... **.**

We are in for the ride of our lives when we surrender to what God has in store for us. Will you embrace your God-given identity and trust His plans for you, or will you refuse to surrender your life to Jesus?

For you did not receive a spirit of slavery to fall back into fear, but you received the Spirit of adoption, by whom we cry out, "Abba, Father!"
—Rom. 8:15

Therefore, we are ambassadors for Christ, certain that God is appealing through us. We plead on Christ's behalf, "Be reconciled to God."
—2 Cor. 5:20

I have treasured Your word in my heart so that I may not sin against You.
—Ps. 119:11

"For I know the plans I have for you"—this is the LORD's declaration— "plans for your welfare, not for disaster, to give you a future and a hope."
—Jer. 29:11

23

What scares you about this <u>God</u>-sized <u>adventure</u>?

Action step

Each week you will be given an action step to help you put into practice what you've learned through your Bible study. This week, you are being challenged to practice living as if your life is not your own. (It's not!) Choose a slot of time in which you are usually free to do what you want (right after school or after your homework is completed). Instead of using that time to focus on yourself, use it to meet a need of someone in your home. Here are a few options (or choose your own):

1. **Offer to cook dinner one evening.** Encourage your parents to spend the time they would have spent cooking and cleaning doing something that helps them relax.

2. **Take your younger brother or sister outside** for some play time. Let him or her pick the game and then play until he or she is worn out. For extra credit, allow a friend of his or hers to hang out with you, too.

3. **Spend 30 minutes in prayer for someone in need.** Don't use this prayer time to make requests for yourself. Concentrate your prayer efforts on the needs of someone else. It could be a person in your church, a teacher, or a family member.

Taking care of the needs of others made me feel...

I realized that submission is...

Reflections of truth

Each week, you will write out one truth you learned this week, then place that truth on a mirror you use regularly. Write your weekly truth on an index card or sticky note or by using a dry erase marker directly on the mirror. Leave your truths up until the completion of the study and watch how it changes what you see in the mirror.

> **Week 1 Truth:**
> **I am the daughter of the King of kings!**
> Romans 8:15-17

*"For you did not receive a spirit of slavery to fall back into fear, but you received the Spirit of adoption, by whom we cry out, "Abba, Father!" The Spirit Him- self testifies together with our spirit that we are God's children, and if children, also heirs—heirs of God and co-heirs with Christ—seeing that we suffer with Him so that we may also be glori- fied with Him."
—Rom. 8:15-17*

1. "Loony Laws," Loony Laws (online). Cited 4 March 2010. Available from the Internet: *www. loonylaws.com.*

WHO is REALLY ON THE THRONE?

First Glance

Picture this scene. The king is sitting on his throne. His appearance is so magnificent that you struggle to find the words to describe him. The entire room is filled with adoring subjects who spend day and night worshiping him. No one is thinking of themselves. All eyes are on the king.

This is the picture that is painted for us of *our* King. The imagery used to describe Him is so bold that it can be difficult to wrap our minds around it. Even so, a closer look at the powerful King shows us who really sits on the throne.

What's your image of the King? How do you envision God's throne room? What is His throne made of? What does God look like when He sits on the throne? Who else is in the throne room? What are they doing?

Write out your description of God's throne room below. If you are better with pictures than words, you may draw the throne room instead.

When we think about God, we don't always consider His role as King. Listed below are several other roles God plays in our lives. Circle the ones that you relate to best.

Friend	Judge	Father	Counselor	Physician
Hero	Provider	Teacher	Shepherd	Truth

Our God is all of the things above, but He is also our powerful King. He is the ruler of the entire world, and He wants to be the ruler of our lives. As we will read together from His Word, when we see the throne room of God, there is no doubt who has the right to reign.

A glimpse of our King

The Book of Revelation provides two powerful images of God as King. In Revelation 4:1-11 we read John's account of a vision given to him during his exile to the island of

Patmos. This vision gives us a glimpse into what heaven is like, but the focus is on the One who sits on the throne.

Read Revelation 4:1-11 out loud as a group.

What a powerful description! There is so much contained in these eleven verses that it can be difficult for our minds to absorb it all. Let's break it down a bit.

Follow the instructions below to take a closer look at this passage.
■ In your Bible, circle the adjectives used to describe what the King looks like.
■ Underline the descriptions of the individuals and creatures that are in the throne room with the King. Put a double line under any description of what they are doing.
■ Highlight descriptions of heaven and the throne room.
■ Put a box around descriptions of what God is like. *(Example: holy)*

If you could describe the King in this passage in one word, what would it be? ....

This image of God on His throne is powerful enough. But a few chapters later, we see a description of our warrior King.

Read Revelation 19:11-16 out loud as a group.

■ List the names of God found in this passage. ....
....

■ What objects described in this passage are typically associated with royalty? List them below. ....
....

■ If you could describe the King in this passage in one word, what would it be? ....

Your role in this story

In a sentence or two, describe how you would feel if you were seated in the room described in Revelation 4:1-11. .....
....
....
....
....

What if you could see the warrior King described in Revelation 19:11-16? What would you say to Him? How would you act in front of Him? Explain your answer below.

You may be struggling with how to behave when faced with this powerful King. My guess is that each of us would follow the lead of the elders and creatures described in the first passage. When confronted with the reality of how powerful our King is, only one reaction would be appropriate—worship. In fact, these passages make it crystal clear what our position is before our powerful King. He is the One on the throne. We are worshipers of God, not the ones being worshiped.

Read Revelation 4:1-11 again with the following questions in mind:

◼ Where are you discussed in this passage?

◼ Where is your throne?

◼ Where is your crown?

◼ Who is worshiping you?

You're not in the throne room. You are not the center of attention. You may be a daughter of the King, but these passages clearly show that God is the One who is *really* on the throne. This perspective should lead you to a place of humility. Your focus should shift from an "all-about-me" mentality to a focus that is all about the King.

Worship your King

Take a moment to worship God creatively. Write out a poem or song lyrics below that focus on how awesome God is. You can return to the passages in this session for inspiration or simply write what you love about your King. Focus your worship on who He is.

PART 1: Who sits on the throne of your heart?

The passages you examined in Revelation are an important reminder of the powerful King we serve. He is worthy of all of our worship and praise. This is easy to remember in the throne room of heaven, but it can be easy to forget in our day-to-day lives. Our tendency is to take God off the throne by the way that we live, the people or things that consume our thoughts, or by the way that we spend our time and talents.

In fact, whether we realize it or not, we decide every day what is most important to us. We put that thing on the throne of our hearts. We crown that most important thing as king. Whatever sits on our heart's throne will rule us.

The tendency to worship something or someone other than God is not new. In fact, it is addressed over and over in the Bible. The Bible repeatedly uses one word to describe those things other than God that sit on the throne in the hearts of God's people.

Any guesses as to what that word is?

If you guessed "idol," you're right on the money. The practice of worshiping idols is addressed more than 200 times in the Bible. God disciplined His people for worshiping physical idols such as a golden calf (Ex. 32:19-35) or statues carved from precious metal (Ps. 115:4). Since we no longer worship statues, passages warning us to avoid the worship of idols may seem irrelevant. But Scripture provides a much broader description of the dangers of idols that applies to the way we live today.

In your own words, write a definition for the word "idol."

Idols don't have to be statues carved from silver or gold. They can be anything that we are devoted to or worship. An idol can even be a way of thinking that is contrary to God's Truth. Regardless of the type of idol, God is serious about removing all kinds of idols from our lives.

Write out the following passages below.

■ Isaiah 42:8 ....

....

....

■ 1 Corinthians 10:14 ....

....

■ 1 John 5:20-21 ....

....

....

What do these passages reveal about God's attitude toward idols? ....

....

What actions do these passages ask us to take when we are tempted to worship something or someone other than God? ....

....

A whale of an idol

Jonah is most famous for the time he spent in the belly of a whale. But he's a great example of an individual who forgot who should sit on the throne and chose to worship his own plans, perceptions, and emotions. Let's examine the consequences of idol worship in Jonah's life.

Read Jonah 1–2.

■ What actions did Jonah take that indicated he had forgotten what a powerful King God is? ....

....

■ What were the immediate consequences of those actions? ....

....

The dictionary defines "idol" this way:
1. an object of worship
2. an object of extreme devotion
3. a false conception[1]

Look at the definitions of "idol" in the left margin. Can you identify the idols in Jonah's life? Circle all that apply.

Himself	Comfort	Security
A golden calf	Pride	False gods
His popularity	The Ninevites	
His own ideas about whom God should save		

Jonah didn't worship false gods. We don't find him bowing down to a golden calf. But he did forget who was in charge. **He forgot that whomever or whatever sits on the throne in his heart is the one with authority over his life.** He ignored God's instructions and took extreme measures to protect himself, his comfort, his pride, his security, and his own ideas about whom God should save. The consequences were huge.

In the belly of the whale, Jonah was reminded who was really on the throne.

Write out Jonah 2:7-9 in the margin. What conclusion did Jonah come to about idols? Go back and circle it in the Scripture you wrote in the margin.

We are all like Jonah. We are all guilty of forgetting how powerful our King is. Despite God's warnings to flee from idols, we put thousands of other things on God's throne. Remember, an idol is anything that we are devoted to or worship. Your idol is whatever you see as the most important thing in your life.

Below is a list of common idols in our culture. Circle the ones that apply to you.

My boyfriend	Popularity	Outer beauty
Material possessions	Sports	Good grades
My youth group	Fashion	Comfort
Facebook®/MySpace	My family	My friends
Plans for the future		

Looking at the idols of others

We are all guilty of placing something or someone other than God on the throne of our hearts. Below are several quotes; many of them are from girls like you.[2]

Underneath each, write down your reaction to the quote. Can you relate to what's being said? Does the quote hit close to home? Does it help you identify a similar idol in your own life? Explain.

"I love swimming! My best friends are all on the swim team, and the pool is my favorite place to be. And you know what? I'm good at it. My coaches tell me I'm good enough to go to college on a swimming scholarship. I have to admit, I get a rush every

time I win a competition. I love hearing the crowd's applause and the affirmation I get from my coaches and parents for a job well done. But lately I've been thinking that swimming doesn't leave me much time for God. Because of practices, I haven't been to youth group in ages, and I am way too tired to read my Bible and pray. I hate to admit it, but swimming has really hurt my relationship with God." —Angie, age 15

"I have to get good grades. If I don't, I won't get any scholarships. If I don't get any scholarships, I won't be able to go to the college I want. If I don't go to college, I won't be able to become an accountant like I've always wanted to. I spend hours every night doing homework. Most of my weekends are spent writing papers or studying for the SAT. There isn't much time left for anything else, but I have to get good grades." —Kelsey, age 17

"I have always felt left out because even my closest friends have boyfriends. I feel like no guy is even looking at me. It's hard being left out and alone. I spend a lot of time daydreaming about having a boyfriend. Some days it's all I think about. I would just feel so much better about myself if a guy was interested in me." —Jaylynn, 14

What's on your throne?

God is the only One worthy to have the complete devotion of our hearts. Jonah's story is a powerful reminder of what happens when we forget who should sit on the throne. When we worship ourselves, our relationships, our activities, or our own interests, there are consequences. We may not find ourselves in the belly of a whale, but we will face hardship when we allow anything other than God to rule our lives.

In what area of your life do you need to place God back on the throne?

Write down a Scripture that encourages you to deal with the idols in your life.

PART 2: Is God a good King?

What characteristics do we value in an earthly king? Consider what makes a good ruler. Rank the following characteristics in order of importance, with 1 being most important and 8 being least important. I want my king to be...

.... Strong   .... Kind   .... Capable   .... Trustworthy
.... Wise   .... Just   .... Powerful   .... Compassionate

Which characteristic did you rank as most important in a king? Why? ....

Which characteristic did you rank as least important in a king? Why? ....

The character of our King

Unlike any earthly ruler, God has *all* of these qualities.

Match the following verses about God with the characteristics listed above in the first activity. Write the matching characteristic beside each Scripture reference.

- Deuteronomy 32:4 ....
- 2 Samuel 7:28 ....
- 2 Chronicles 20:6 ....
- Psalm 86:15 ....
- Proverbs 18:10 ....
- Isaiah 63:7 ....
- 1 Corinthians 1:25 ....
- 2 Corinthians 9:8 ....

Because earthly rulers are human, they cannot be *everything* we desire in a king. It can be difficult to find a ruler who is both powerful and kind, loving and strong, just and compassionate. Because of this, the idea of surrendering our lives to a human king seems crazy. But God is a capable King. We can trust Him with our lives because He has what it takes to rule.

A lesson from Job

When life gets tough, we tend to turn our focus inward. We can get pretty wrapped up in what is happening in our own lives and forget that we serve a King who is powerful enough to handle our circumstances. This was certainly true in Job's life. Job is famous for the trials he faced. Job's servants and sheep were burned up in a fire (Job 1:16); his camels were taken by a raiding party (1:17); all ten of his children were killed (1:18-19). Job was inflicted with painful sores from the soles of his feet to the top of his head (2:7-8). His wife told him to "curse God and die" (2:9). Later, a group of his friends showed up and hinted that Job brought this all on himself.

What would you be feeling if you were Job?

How would such devastating losses change how you felt about God?

Most of us would respond by asking the same question: "Why me?" Our natural response would be to focus on ourselves. Facing a tragedy of this magnitude would make us feel powerless. When we feel powerless, it can be difficult to see how powerful God is.

God eventually spoke to Job. But He did not offer an explanation for Job's circumstances that were Job-focused. Instead, God offered a powerful reminder of what kind of ruler He is.

Read Job 38–39. Write down in the margin the phrases that remind you of how powerful God is.

God wasn't tooting His own horn in these chapters. He didn't have to. He was reminding Job who sits on the throne. It didn't take long for Job's "all-about-me" attitude to shift. In Job 40:3-5 we see that Job realized what a powerful God he served.

In the closing chapters, God reminded Job of His power. He wasn't rubbing salt in Job's wounds. He wasn't kicking Job while he was down. God was simply reminding Job who's in charge. More importantly, God knew that Job needed to know he served a God powerful enough to handle Job's most difficult circumstances.

Then Job answered the LORD: I am so insignificant. How can I answer You? I place my hand over my mouth. I have spoken once, and I will not reply; twice, but now I can add nothing."
—Job 40:3-5

Your Job moment

Describe a time when you faced some very difficult circumstances.

■ How did you react to those circumstances? What were your actions? What were your feelings?

....

....

■ How did you treat others during that time?

....

....

■ How did you feel about God during that trial?

....

....

■ What was your relationship with God like in that time?

....

We serve a powerful and capable King. He can handle the throne. But He is more than powerful. He is also good. This can be difficult to remember when your friend's mom is diagnosed with cancer or your parents are getting a divorce. When your best friends abandon you or life doesn't work out the way you planned, it can be easy to lose perspective. You may realize that God is capable of changing your circumstances, but when He doesn't, you may doubt that He is a good King. When your emotions deceive you in this way, it is important to cling to God's Truth.

Write out the following verses in your own words below.

■ Psalm 84:11

....

■ Matthew 7:9-11

....

■ Romans 8:28

....

■ James 1:17

....

....

We serve a good God. He is able and willing to give good gifts to His children. The fact that we serve a good and powerful King should shape the way that we live and respond to our circumstances.

Fill in the chart below with verses that remind you of the character of your King. You can use the passages from this study or find your own.

WHEN . . .	GOD IS . . .
I feel afraid	
I am arguing with my family	
I am sick	
My friends ditch me	
I am stressed	
My heart is broken	

Second Look

PART 3: Our approachable King

 Quiz: *Are you approachable?*

Are people drawn to you or are you secretly sending the signal to "buzz off?"
■ When you catch someone looking at you, you usually react by:
   a) making eye contact and smiling
   b) striking up a conversation
   c) refusing to make eye contact

■ The new girl at school is always stopping at your locker to chat, you:
   a) make small talk with her while you get books you need but get to class ASAP
   b) let her talk, even if it means getting another tardy in algebra
   c) act like you don't see her and run when you see her approaching

■ You're in an elevator with a teacher from school. You:
   a) smile once and spend the next three floors looking at the wall
   b) start a conversation about what's going on in school
   c) lock your eyes on the buttons and don't say a word

■ A new girl comes to youth group. Your youth pastor asks you to make her feel welcome. Your response is:
   a) "I don't mind, as long as I have my friends with me."
   b) "Absolutely! I love to meet new people."
   c) "No way! Meeting new people makes my stomach hurt."

■ Your youth pastor chooses you to represent the youth group on a new committee at church. At the first meeting, you realize you don't know a soul. You:
   a) Find an empty chair and introduce yourself to the lady next to you, but only answer direct questions during the meeting.
   b) Use the time before the meeting starts to meet other people in the room. You feel comfortable contributing your thoughts throughout the meeting.
   c) Grab a chair in the corner and make a mental note to ask your youth pastor to send someone else to the next meeting.

Check your answers to see how many As, Bs, and Cs you have.

Mostly As. You're generally easy to talk to and friendly. Strangers would pick up on the fact that it's OK to stop you to ask for directions, but you're not likely to initiate a conversation with a stranger.

Mostly Bs. People flock to you like moths to a flame. You don't know a stranger and seize every opportunity to meet someone new. Your outgoing nature can get you into trouble since everyone sees you as a potential BFF and your tendency to talk can frustrate others in class or at church. You love being with people!

Mostly Cs. You don't mean to, but you tend to send a "buzz off" vibe. Meeting new people always makes you nervous. You've had the same best friend since second grade, and you like it that way. Others would describe you as loyal and a good listener, but you won't be voted "most outgoing" any time soon.

Someone who's approachable might also be described as accessible and friendly. Approachability is an important quality to possess if you're looking to make new friends, but it isn't a quality we often associate with royalty. Kings tend to be pretty picky about whom they allow to approach their throne. Interactions with the king require a royal invitation.

As we've already learned, our God isn't like most kings. We've considered His goodness and power, but it is worthwhile to ask: Is our King approachable? There's no doubt that He sits on a mighty throne, but is He accessible?

Esther approached her king

The biblical story of Esther paints an elaborate picture of royalty. Esther's entire story is contained in 10 short chapters.

Take the time to read the entire story in the Book of Esther in your Bible.

■ What's your favorite part about this story?
....

■ Who's your favorite character in this story? Why?
....

■ What kind of king is described in this story?
....

The story of Esther is one of my favorites because it sounds so much like a fairy tale. King Xerxes (or Ahasuerus) needs to select a new queen. Esther is chosen from among all of the eligible women of the land because of her beauty. A villain enters. Conflict arises. The queen's people are threatened. Love wins. The story even ends with a happily ever after. The queen and her family are spared, and the bad guy meets his doom. Walt Disney himself couldn't have written a better plot!

Esther is both the beauty and the heroine we find in so many fairy tales. But she didn't serve an approachable king.

She was not allowed to see the king unless he summoned her by name (Esth. 2:14). In fact, anyone who approached this king without an invitation faced almost certain death.

Esther knew that her people, the Jews, faced annihilation by the order of the king. She knew that her family was counting on her to speak up on their behalf. But she also knew that King Xerxes was virtually inaccessible.

What was Esther's first response when Mordecai asked her to approach the king on behalf of the Jews?

■ Summarize her words (found in Esth. 4:11).

....

....

■ What could happen to Esther if she approached the king uninvited?..

Gulp! If Esther bucked protocol and approached the king uninvited, she could be killed. This law was created to communicate that the power of King Xerxes was absolute. He was the one in charge. He wasn't worried about appearing approachable.

But Esther approached him anyway. In chapter 5, our heroine went to her king without a royal invitation.

How do you think Esther was feeling in the moments before she entered the inner court?..

What motivated her to approach her unapproachable king?..

....

Esther knew the stakes. She understood who was in charge, but in order to save her people, she ignored the rules and entered the throne room.

We already know what happened next. The king held out the scepter. Esther's life was spared. Over and over throughout the rest of the book, Esther was allowed to approach the king, and her requests were granted.

Why? The answer is found in Esther 5:2a: "As soon as the king saw Queen Esther standing in the courtyard, *she won his approval.*"

King Xerxes didn't suddenly decide to become a more approachable king. He wasn't worried about his image. He spared Esther because he was pleased with her. He granted her requests because he loved her. There is a lesson in this story about our own King.

WHEN GOD DOESN'T SEEM TO ANSWER
Keep these four principles in mind when God's response to your prayers doesn't meet your expectations.
1. God's ways are not our ways (Isa. 55:8-9).
2. We can trust God to work things out for our good (Rom. 8:28).
3. Keep praying (1 Thess. 5:16-18)!
4. Even when our prayers aren't answered in the way that we'd like, God has promised us peace (Phil. 4:6-7).

Approach His throne with confidence

In Hebrews 4:14-16, we find a description of our King that answers the approachability question. **Write out the passage in the margin to the left.**

God has extended the golden scepter to us. He has invited us into the throne room. He is our approachable King. **Go back and circle the word that describes how we are encouraged to approach God's throne.**

The Bible urges us to approach the throne with *confidence* or *boldness*. Unlike Esther, we don't have to worry about how our King will react to our presence. We have no reason to believe that something bad will happen to us if we seek our King. He invites us to approach. Why? Because of His great love for us.

How to approach our King

There are many ways we can encounter God. We can experience Him through worship; we can get to know Him through His Word; and we can approach Him through prayer. And this is the great truth: God doesn't just tolerate our prayers. He encourages us to seek Him through prayer. He *wants* us to approach His throne and talk with Him. What's more, our King does more than hear our prayers. He responds to them. James 5:16b promises, *"The urgent request of a righteous person is very powerful..."*

Let's go back to Esther's story. Against huge odds, Esther changed the mind of her king. Why? Because the king loved her. The same is true of our King. He hears our prayers. He responds to our petitions and praises. Why? Because of His deep love for us. This is why we are able to approach God's throne with confidence. You have probably already seen this truth played out in your own life.

Below, reflect on times when God responded to your prayers. If He has not yet answered your prayer in an area, leave "God's response" blank and fill it in later.

Your prayer   **God's response**
A prayer for yourself...
A prayer for a friend...
A prayer for physical healing.......................................
A prayer for someone's salvation..............................
A prayer for guidance...

When God doesn't seem to answer

It's true that we serve a God who listens and responds to prayer. We can be confident that when we pray, we are heard. Our prayers don't just float around in the stratosphere. But our God isn't required to give us everything we want when we want it. Because He is our sovereign King, He may not respond to our prayers in the way we want Him to or according to our timing. But we can trust Him to answer prayers with our best interests and His glory in mind.

Summing it all up

Here's a quick summary of what you've learned this week.

1. God is my .... My role is to .... , not to be the one ....

God alone is worthy to be <u>King</u> and is worthy of our <u>worship</u>. Today's culture may tell us differently, but the truth is that we are *not* the ones to be <u>worshiped</u>.

2. Whatever is most important to me will become my ....

Read Isaiah 42:8. Every day we decide what is most important to us. As we learned from Jonah, when we forget who sits on the throne and worship something other than God (an <u>idol</u>), the results are disastrous.

3. When my circumstances are difficult, it's important to remember that I serve a .... King.

God is more than a powerful King. He is also a <u>good</u> King. His Word shows us that He is kind and compassionate and has good things in mind for His children.

4. I can approach God's throne with .... through ....

Hebrews 4:16 says, *"Therefore let us approach the throne of grace with <u>boldness</u>, so that we may receive mercy and find grace to help us at the proper time."*

"Our Lord and God, You are worthy to receive glory and honor and power, because You have created all things, and because of Your will they exist and were created."
—Rev. 4:11

"I am Yahweh, that is My name; I will not give My glory to another, or my praise to idols."
—Isa. 42:8

"I will make known the LORD's faithful love and the LORD's praise-worthy acts, because of all the Lord has done for us— even the many good things He has done for the house of Israel and has done for them based on His compassion and the abundance of His faithful love."
—Isa. 63:7

God is more than a good, powerful, and capable King. He's also approachable. He invites us to come to Him because He loves us. We can approach God any time through <u>prayer</u>. Through His Word, God promises to listen and respond when we pray.

Action step

Each week you will be given an action step that will help you put into practice what you've learned through your group and individual Bible study. This week, **recruit a prayer partner.** God invites us to approach Him, but we often find ourselves too busy to take Him up on His offer. Work on strengthening this discipline in your life with the help of a friend. Find someone you can count on to pray with you. Make plans to pray together at least once over the next week. Or you could meet daily over the phone or before school to pray together.

My prayer partner is: ....

We are going to meet .... **to pray.**

My prayer requests are: ....
....

My partner's prayer requests are: ....
....

Reflections of truth

Each week, you will write out one truth you learned this week, then place that truth on a mirror you use regularly. Write your weekly truth on an index card or sticky note or by using a dry erase marker directly on the mirror. Leave your truths up until the completion of the study and watch how it changes what you see in the mirror.

Week 2 Truth:
I worship a powerful King!
Revelation 4:11

"Our Lord and God, You are worthy to receive glory and honor and power, because You have created all things, and because of Your will they exist and were created."
—Rev. 4:11

1. "Idol," Merriam-Webster Online Dictionary. Cited 5 March 2010. Available from the Internet: *http://www.merriam-webster.com/dictionary/idol*
2. Author's interviews with students, [December 2009]. All interviews were held in confidentiality, and the names of interviewees have been changed by mutual agreement.

ROYALTY REDEFINED

First Glance

When a king has a message to send, how does he usually send it?

In the story of Cinderella, Prince Charming needed to find a wife, so the king sent out invitations to a royal ball. Second Samuel 11:19-25 tells us that King David sent a messenger to give orders to his troops during battle. In Esther 3:13, King Xerxes relied on couriers to carry out his royal edict.

We are accustomed to hearing royal messengers make announcements on behalf of the king. But Christ is no ordinary King. He rarely does things the way other kings do. This is especially true when He has a message to send.

Redefining royalty

In earthly kingdoms, the king sends a messenger. The king's edicts are announced by messengers proclaiming "Hear ye, Hear ye." But this wasn't how *our* King sent a message. He didn't send a messenger. He sent Himself. Jesus was the *message* and the *Messenger.*

It's important to ask ourselves a key question*: Why did He come to earth at all? Why would this King take off His royal robes and walk among the common?*

He become flesh and blood because our King wanted us to hear His powerful message straight from Him.

The message arrives

The following verse describes how God's message was delivered to us through Jesus. In each blank, fill in a synonym for the word(s) provided in parentheses.

- " .... (The Word) became .... (flesh) and .... (made his dwelling) among .... (us). We observed his .... (glory), the glory as the (One and Only) Son from .... (the Father), full of .... (grace) and .... (truth). —John 1:14

- Who does "the Word" describe in this passage? ....

Remember, the Word of God is one of the names given to Jesus (Rev. 19:13). That same passage also describes Jesus as the King of kings. When we connect the dots, we see that John 1:14 is describing a truly unique event—Jesus, the King of kings, became a Man and lived among His people!

This Truth becomes even more amazing as we examine the *way* our King arrived.

Read Luke 2:1-20. Describe Jesus' arrival on earth in a single word.

Jesus couldn't have arrived under more humble circumstances. There was no grand entry. No trumpets blaring or banners waving. No heralds announcing the arrival. Instead, Jesus came as a helpless baby. He was born into the arms of poor parents who had nowhere else to put Him but a trough intended for livestock feed.

Why do you think Jesus chose to come to earth in this way?

The shepherds came to the manger in search of a Savior (Luke 2:8-16). What do you think they felt when they found Jesus in a stable?

Everything about Jesus' arrival sent a message. What do you think the message was? What does the message mean to you?

The shepherds were among the first to hear the message that Jesus came to bring. Go back and read Luke 2:10-11. Use that passage to fill in the blanks below.

■ Jesus came to earth to bring _____ news to _____ people. The good news is that He is our _____.

Our King didn't just come to rescue a few. News of His arrival didn't stop with the shepherds. Jesus came to bring **good** news to **all** people. The good news is that our King came to earth to be our **Savior.** But what did He come to save us from?

Look up the following Scriptures. Then, list beside each one the phrases that describe what our King came to save us from.

■ Matthew 1:21

■ Romans 5:9-11

■ 2 Timothy 1:8-10

■ Romans 6:23

The passages describe the state of the kingdom (earth) before Jesus came. Jews and Gentiles (which means all of us!) needed a permanent remedy for our sin problem. We needed to be saved from the spiritual death that sin inevitably brings. When things were getting bad in the kingdom, God didn't just send a message through a secretary. He didn't use couriers to announce a royal edict. He came Himself with a message of hope because He was the message we needed.

Now it's your turn to be the messenger. Announce Christ's arrival and His message in the form of a royal proclamation.

Hear ye, Hear ye...

Christ's message didn't stop at the manger. That was just the beginning! Jesus continued to send a powerful message by the way that He lived and the way that He died. His example redefines royalty, and He calls us to follow that example.

PART 1: How did He come?

We've already taken a peek at Christ's arrival on earth. Now let's dig a little deeper. The story of Mary, the shepherds, and the manger is likely a familiar one to you. But it is so much more than a story told only at Christmas. Jesus' birth has a lot to teach us about the kind of King we serve and the way we should live out our role as daughters of the King.

Read Matthew 1:1-17. Write down the names of any kings listed in this passage. ....

You probably didn't know that this passage actually contains the names of 15 kings! Beginning with King David and ending with Jeconiah, the lineage of Christ is jam-packed with royal ancestors.

   The first two chapters of the Book of Matthew describe Jesus' birth. But Matthew didn't start by writing about the manger. He didn't begin with Joseph's discovery that his fiancée (who was a virgin) was pregnant. He didn't even open the story with the announcement of Mary's visit from the angel. Instead, he began the story of Jesus' arrival by listing the heritage of Christ.

Why do you think Matthew opened the story this way? .....

....

....

While it may not interest you to read a long list of names like the one found in Matthew 1:1-17, it's important not to miss the writer's point. This passage proves Jesus' royal heritage. All kings must come from an authentic lineage. They need to prove that they are descendants of royalty. These verses prove that Jesus was born from the line of King David. His credentials check out. In order to fully understand the message of Jesus, we need to realize that He is truly a King in the literal sense of the word.

   Jesus was royal, but His birth certainly was not. Two royal birth announcements follow. First is the announcement of Jesus' birth found in Luke 2:1-18. Second is an excerpt of *People* magazine's announcement of England's Prince Harry's 1984 birth.

Announcing King Jesus!

"In those days a decree went out from Caesar Augustus that the whole empire should be registered. This first registration took place while Quirinius was governing Syria. So everyone went to be registered, each to his own town.

And Joseph also went up from the town of Nazareth in Galilee, to Judea, to the city of David, which is called Bethlehem, because he was of the house and family line of David, to be registered along with Mary, who was engaged to him and was pregnant. While they were there, the time came for her to give birth. Then she gave birth to her firstborn Son, and she wrapped Him snugly in cloth and laid Him in a feeding trough—because there was no room for them at the lodging place.

In the same region, shepherds were staying out in the fields and keeping watch at night over their flock. Then an angel of the Lord stood before them, and the glory of the Lord shone around them, and they were terrified. But the angel said to them, 'Don't be afraid, for look, I proclaim to you good news of great joy that will be for all the people: Today a Savior, who is Messiah the Lord, was born for you in the city of David. This will be the sign for you: you will find a baby wrapped snugly in cloth and lying in a feeding trough.'

Suddenly there was a multitude of the heavenly host with the angel, praising God and saying: 'Glory to God in the highest heaven, and peace on earth to people He favors!'

When the angels had left them and returned to heaven, the shepherds said to one another, 'Let's go straight to Bethlehem and see what has happened, which the Lord has made known to us.'

They hurried off and found both Mary and Joseph, and the baby who was lying in the feeding trough. After seeing them, they reported the message they were told about this child, and all who heard it were amazed at what the shepherds said to them."

Announcing Prince Harry!

"Outside St. Mary's Hospital in the slightly shabby London section of Paddington, the crowd was growing by the minute—more than 300 reporters, TV technicians and curious onlookers milled anxiously behind a double row of police barricades and dozens of photographers and TV cameramen perched atop ladders nearby. Inside the hospital, in the private wing, Diana, Princess of Wales, had been in labor since 7:30 a.m. Finally after nine hours, as the afternoon light began to fade and a gray sky threatened rain, a son emerged for all of Britain. Fair of face and blue-eyed like his brother, William, he weighed in at six pounds, 14 ounces. The infant, third in line to the throne after his father and brother, would be known officially as Prince Henry Charles Albert David, it was announced—and just "Harry" to his family and chums. A TV crewman, hooked up to his home office through head-phones, broke the news to the mob outside St. Mary's. "It's a boy!" he shouted. The crowd exploded in cheers...

Moments later a town crier, decked out in a white-plumed hat and red knickers, rang a large bronze bell and intoned, "Her Royal Highness the Princess Diana has issued forth a second son." ...Champagne corks popped and church bells pealed throughout the kingdom. Congratulatory flowers and telegrams poured into the hospital, and two traditional 41-gun salutes ripped the air. One was fired in Hyde Park by the Queen's Troop, the Royal Horse Artillery. A second salute was fired simultaneously from the Tower of London."[1]

Compare these events by answering the questions below.

	JESUS' BIRTH	HARRY'S BIRTH
Where was the baby born?		
How many people attended the birth?		
What was the mood at the time of the birth?		
How did others react to news of the birth?		
What exact words were used to announce the arrival of the baby?		
Describe the birth in one word:		

Humility and meekness

Two themes are present throughout the story of Jesus' birth—humility and meekness.

Circle the best definition of these two terms from the lists below.

■ Humility is...
   a) The state of being humble or not proud
   b) Thinking poorly of yourself
   c) The opposite of expensive or luxurious
   d) Allowing others to treat you badly

Answers a and c both correctly define the word *humility.* **Which of those two definitions best describes our King?**

■ Meekness is...
   a) Being gentle and kind
   b) Enduring injury with patience and without resentment
   c) To be mild
   d) Submitting to others

All of these definitions accurately define the quality of **meekness.** To be meek isn't the same as being weak. Meekness means being mild, gentle, and kind. It is strength under control. All of the major characters involved in the story of Jesus' birth, including the King Himself, modeled humility and meekness.

Use the chart below to record examples of these two qualities in the lives of those who responded to Jesus' birth.

	Demonstrated humility by...	Demonstrated meekness by...
Jesus		
Mary (Luke 1:26-38)		
Joseph (Matthew 1:18-25)		
Magi (Matthew 2:1-12)		
Shepherds (Luke 2:8-20)		

Meekness and humility remained important themes throughout Jesus' life and ministry. He modeled these qualities first and then asked us to follow His example. In fact, He offers many promises to those who live in humility and meekness. Match the verses below with the promise given.

Bible Verse	God's Promise
Matthew 5:5	Inherit the land/Earth
Matt. 23:12	Enjoy great peace
Proverbs 3:34	He will lift you up
James 4:10	He will exalt you/lift you up
Psalm 37:11	He will give you grace

Think about it

Go back and review the definitions of meekness and humility.

■ Do you think these qualities are valued by the world? Explain.

■ Is it easy or difficult to model meekness and humility in your life? Explain.

■ What is one way you can practice not being proud this week?

■ What is one way you can practice strength under control this week?

51

Second Look

For a child will be born for us, a son will be given to us, and the government will be on His shoulders. He will be named Wonderful Counselor, Mighty God, Eternal Father, Prince of Peace. The dominion will be vast, and its prosperity will never end. He will reign on the throne of David and over his kingdom, to establish and sustain it with justice and righteousness from now on and forever. The zeal of the LORD of Hosts will accomplish this.
—Isa. 9:6-7

PART 2: How did He live?

During Jesus' time on earth, He was fully man but remained fully God. He never removed His crown. He never abdicated His throne. He walked among His people as King. But like His birth, His life didn't look very royal. The Jews were expecting a king. The prophet Isaiah had foretold that a ruler was coming.

Based on Isaiah 9:6-7 (in the margin to the left), what kind of king do you think the Jews were expecting? Describe him below.

Even though the people had long hoped for the kind of king Isaiah described, they misunderstood Jesus' mission and actions. They eagerly waited for a king who would rescue them from political domination, but when He arrived without a physical crown or throne, they were baffled. They were confused by His humble appearance and circumstances. They didn't understand the source of His power and wisdom. They didn't get why He allowed Himself to be beaten and hung on a cross. But their image of royalty was most shaken by the fact that Jesus lived more like a servant than a king. He didn't force others to serve Him; instead He consistently practiced a life of service.

According to Matthew 20:25-28 (in the margin on the next page), what is the difference between a king and a servant?

What did Jesus mean when He said that to become great we must be a servant?

Write three examples from Jesus' life that prove His claim that He "did not come to be served, but to serve."

Jesus' example of servanthood is perhaps most clearly modeled just prior to the last supper. Jesus washed the feet of His disciples. In this single act, the humility of Jesus collided with His servant's heart. He modeled unglamorous service to others, and His example urges us to do the same.

Read John 13:1-17. Imagine that you are among the disciples that night. It's your turn to have your feet washed by the Savior. As He removes your sandals and begins to gently wash the mud and grime from your feet...

■ What expression does Jesus have on His face?

■ What are you feeling?

■ What do you want to say to Jesus?

■ What is He teaching you about service to others?

Jesus washed the disciples' feet because they were dirty. The disciples wore sandals and traveled along unpaved roads. It was a yucky job, one we wouldn't expect a King to carry out; yet, Jesus washed His friends' feet. It wasn't a ceremony. It was an act of service.

If we are going to live out Jesus' redefinition of royalty, we need to catch His vision of service. He lived a life of service that put others first, which often meant getting His hands dirty and taking care of others at inconvenient times. As daughters of the King, we are called to follow His lead.

Working on your serve

Do you serve others by putting their needs ahead of your own? How well do you serve people around you? For each of the following groups, give yourself a grade for service.

■ my friends
■ my parents
■ the sick
■ strangers
■ my siblings
■ my enemies

■ people younger than me
■ people older than me
■ the poor in my community
■ other members of my church
■ the unchurched
■ orphans

But Jesus called them over and said, "You know that the rulers of the Gentiles dominate them, and the men of high position exercise power over them. It must not be like that among you. On the contrary, whoever wants to become great among you must be your servant, and whoever wants to be first among you must be your slave; just as the Son of Man did not come to be served, but to serve, and to give His life— a ransom for many." —Matt. 20:25-28

Do nothing out of rivalry or conceit, but in humility consider others as more important than yourselves. Everyone should look out not only for his own interests, but also for the interests of others.
—Phil. 2:3-4

You may do well at putting the needs of some people ahead of your own (like your best friends), but you may fall short when you have the chance to serve someone you don't know or don't like. Jesus served His closest friends as well as complete strangers. He sought to meet the needs of those who had their act together and those who were needy and desperate. Serving others isn't ceremonial. It isn't something we do when we're in a good mood. We can't check "service" off of our to-do list after participating in a summer mission trip. Jesus modeled a *lifestyle* of service. We are challenged to do the same.

Go back to the list of people on the previous page. Spend some time praying about whom God wants you to serve this week. After you've prayed, choose seven people or groups to focus on, one each day over the next week. Write down next to each person or group the day you will serve them. Next, brainstorm a list of "foot washing" activities you can put into practice as you serve. Remember, Jesus didn't wash the disciples' feet as a ceremony. He did it to meet a practical need. Here are some examples to get you started:

■ Drive my siblings to school to give my mom a break
■ Give my allowance to a local homeless shelter
■ Read stories to sick children at a local hospital
■ Spend an evening playing games with my siblings instead of chatting with friends online

Write about your experiences in the space below.

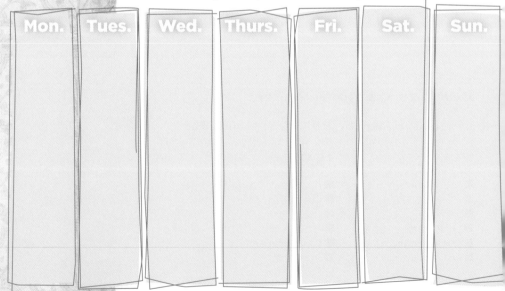

Mon. | Tues. | Wed. | Thurs. | Fri. | Sat. | Sun.

PART 3: How did He die?

Indicate whether you agree or disagree with the following statements.

- ▪ .... "Jesus was the greatest religious genius that ever lived." —Ernest Renan
- ▪ .... "I believe that what people call God is something in all of us. I believe that what Jesus and Mohammed and Buddha and all the rest said was right. It's just that the translations have gone wrong." —John Lennon
- ▪ .... "A man who was completely innocent offered himself as a sacrifice for the good of others, including his enemies, and became the ransom of the world. It was a perfect act." —Mahatma Gandhi
- ▪ .... "Jesus Christ was an extremist for love, truth, and goodness." —Martin Luther King Jr.
- ▪ .... "As the centuries pass, the evidence is accumulating that, measured by His effect on history, Jesus is the most influential life ever lived on this planet." —Kenneth Scott Latourette

Our faith as Christians hinges on one question: Who is Jesus? Is He simply a religious genius or an influential personality from history? Was He a political extremist or a profound spiritual teacher like Mohammed or Buddha? Or is He something much more meaningful? Do His life and death hold eternal significance?

Jesus is so much more than just a good man or a likeable character from history. No description of our King would be complete without examining His death and its impact on our lives. As we study how we should live as daughters of the King by examining His example, we can't stop at the manger or at the last supper. We must follow Him all the way to the cross. Jesus came to model humility, meekness, and service, but ultimately He came to sacrifice His life on the cross as payment for *our* sins.

Read John 19. As you read, write down the emotions that you think Jesus was feeling. ....

....

HIS SACRIFICE
The Bible tells us that Jesus chose to die on the cross as a sacrifice for our sins. Read the verses below and answer the questions that accompany each verse.

Romans 3:23
Who has sinned?

Does that include you?

Romans 6:23
What is the punishment for sin?

In contrast, what gift does God give us through Jesus?

Romans 3:23-26; 1 John 2:2
What does the word "atonement" (or "propitiation") mean?

What did Jesus atone for?

(cont. on p. 56)

55

Hebrews 10:10
What does "holy" or "sanctified" mean?

According to this passage, how have we been made holy?

Fill in the blanks to sum up the truths from these passages.

I am a ....
Because of my ...., I deserve ...., and cannot begin to measure up to God's ....
But Jesus paid the ultimate .... by His .... on the .... so that I could .... and be made ....

Remember, Jesus was fully human during His time on earth. He didn't supernaturally escape the pain and agony that would accompany the scenes you just read. Because He remained fully God, He could have stopped the process at any moment, but He did not. He endured the betrayal, public humiliation, torture, and eventually death.

What motivated Jesus to suffer in this way? ....
....
....

From our human perspective, it doesn't make sense that the King of kings would choose such a horrible and humiliating death. No other king would sign up for betrayal, torture, and death. But our King did. Why? Because such a sacrifice was necessary to rescue us from our own sin.

Follow His lead

You and I will never be able to replicate the sacrifice of Jesus. But as daughters of the King, we do need to make sacrifices. We can follow His example by seeking to meet the needs of others. This is exactly what God calls us to do through His Word. In each of the following verses, circle how we are to live out the principle of sacrifice.

> *Therefore, brothers, by the mercies of God, I urge you to present your bodies as a living sacrifice, holy and pleasing to God; this is your spiritual worship.* —Romans 12:1

> *Therefore, through Him let us continually offer up to God a sacrifice of praise, that is, the fruit of our lips that confess His name. Don't neglect to do what is good and to share, for God is pleased with such sacrifices.* —Hebrews 13:15-16

> *Therefore, be imitators of God, as dearly loved children. And walk in love, as the Messiah also loved us and gave Himself for us, a sacrificial and fragrant offering to God.* —Ephesians 5:1-2

Stories of sacrifice

Sacrifice isn't a popular word in our culture. We hear a lot about greed, but not much about sacrifice. But sacrifice isn't as scary as it sounds. Check out these stories of sacrifices made by girls[2] like you. After each story, write your reaction to what you read. What sticks with you about each story? What is the impact of each girl's sacrifice?

"Every Sunday I volunteer in the nursery at my church. Sure, that means I don't get to be in Sunday School with my friends. It also means that I can't sleep in on Sunday mornings because people are counting on me to be there. But it really is worth the cost. I love the opportunity to tell little ones about Jesus. It's hard work, but it's more rewarding than I ever thought it would be." —Kelly, age 18

....

....

....

"I just broke up with my boyfriend. He didn't do anything wrong. In fact, I'm crazy about him, but it's not the right time for me to be in that kind of relationship. I am nowhere near ready to be married, and giving my heart away so young just made things complicated. If I were being honest with myself, I'd have to admit that I was putting my relationship with my boyfriend ahead of my relationship with Jesus. That isn't where I want to be. I just got the sense that God was asking me to shift my focus back toward Him and trust Him to bring the right guy into my life at the right time. It hurts, but I know it's the right thing to do." —Sara, age 14

....

....

....

"I just sponsored a child in Guatemala through an organization at my church. This is a way I can demonstrate the love of Jesus to someone who really needs it. But $30 a month is a lot of money for me. I will have to make some sacrifices to keep my commitment. My friends and I are going to carpool to school, I've cut out Starbucks runs, and I won't be going to the mall any time soon. But it's worth it. When I think of how far that money will go for that child, all of that stuff seems pretty silly anyway." —Kate, age 16

....

....

....

"It's my senior year, and my plans for the future just got thrown out the window. On a recent retreat I felt God calling me to reach out to people who are sick from cancer. I was planning to become a writer. A career in the medical field wasn't even on my radar screen. But God broke my heart for those who are really sick by showing me Matthew 10:8 which says, "Heal the sick, raise the dead, cleanse those who have leprosy, drive out demons. Freely you have received, freely give." I am called to freely give to others

because I have freely received so much from Jesus. I've already withdrawn from the college I was planning to attend and am looking at options for nursing school. It feels scary, but I am really excited to live out a God-sized adventure." —Nikki, age 18

"I am not a morning person. But lately I've been getting up before the sun rises. I've been a Christian for a long time, but my walk with Christ has always been sort of dull. I knew I needed to get serious about spending time in prayer and personal Bible study, but I just couldn't find the time. Then I saw a poster at church that said "In the morning, O Lord, you hear my voice; in the morning I lay my requests before you and wait in expectation" (Ps. 5:3). I realized that I could spend my mornings with Jesus even if it meant a little less sleep. I'm still not a morning person. It takes effort every morning to drag myself out of bed and open my Bible, but it really is making a difference. My faith is growing and growing, and God is teaching me so much." —Bekah, age 16

Write your story

In what areas is God calling you to make sacrifices? Maybe it's a relationship that needs to end. Maybe you need to sacrifice your pride and say, "I'm sorry." Maybe God is calling you to do something with your time that focuses on the needs of others, or maybe He is calling you to use your money to invest in ministry. Ask God to show you how you can follow Jesus' example of sacrifice, and then answer the questions that follow.

How do you sense God asking you to make a sacrifice?

What fears do you have about that sacrifice?

What Scriptures can you find to confirm what you sense God is calling you to do? Write them in the margin.

What is one step you can take today toward living more sacrificially?

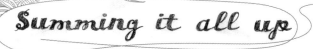

Summing it all up

Here's a quick summary of what you've learned this week.

1. Jesus is the _____ **and the** _____ .

Read Luke 2:10-11. God didn't send someone else when He had a message to send. He became the <u>message</u> and the <u>Messenger</u>. Jesus is our Savior who came to save us from our sins. The way that He came, the way that He lived, and the way that He died completely redefined royalty.

2. Jesus' birth teaches us the value of _____
and _____ .

Read Matthew 5:5. <u>Humility</u> means to be humble, and <u>meekness</u> is best defined as strength under control. These aren't qualities we often see in kings, but they do describe Jesus' birth and life during His time on earth. As daughters of the King, we are called to demonstrate these qualities in the way that we live.

3. Jesus met the needs of others by living a life of
_____ .

Read Matthew 20:26b-28. Living like a daughter of the King means seeking to meet the needs of others through <u>service</u>. A great example of service can be found in the story of Jesus washing the disciples' feet. Jesus didn't wash His friends' feet as a ceremony; He did it to meet a practical need.

4. Jesus' death was an act of _____ **on my behalf.**

Read Hebrews 10:10. Jesus willingly chose to die a painful death in order to pay the price for our sin. We will never be able to match His <u>sacrifice</u>, but we can begin to live more sacrificially.

But the angel said to them, "Don't be afraid, for look, I proclaim to you good news of great joy that will be for all the people: Today a Savior, who is Messiah the Lord, was born for you in the city of David."
—Luke 2:10-11

"Blessed are the meek, for they will inherit the earth."
—Matt. 5:5 (NIV)

"Whoever wants to become great among you must be your servant, and whoever wants to be first among you must be your slave; just as the Son of Man did not come to be served, but to serve."
—Matt.20:26b-28a

By this will of God, we have been sanctified through the offering of the body of Jesus Christ once and for all.
—Heb. 10:10

Action step

Each week you will be given an action step that will help you put into practice what you've learned through your Bible study. This week you will complete your action step with your large group at your next group session.

Reflections of truth

Each week, you will write out one truth you learned this week, then place that truth on a mirror you use regularly. Write your weekly truth on an index card or sticky note or by using a dry erase marker directly on the mirror. Leave your truths up until the completion of the study and watch how it changes what you see in the mirror.

> **Week 3 Truth:**
> **Jesus calls me to live a life of humility.**
> 1 Thessalonians 5:9-10

For God did not appoint us to wrath, but to obtain salvation through our Lord Jesus Christ, who died for us, so that whether we are awake or asleep, we will live together with Him.
—1 Thess. 5:9-10

1. Gioia Diliberto, "Hello, Harry!," *People (online).* 1 October, 1984 [cited 27 April 2010]. Available from the Internet: *http://www.people.com/people/archive/article/0,,20088780,00.html.*
2. Author's interviews with students [December 2009]. All interviews were held in confidentiality, and the names of interviewees have been changed by mutual agreement.

THIS PRESENT KINGDOM

First Glance

Jesus isn't the only One who seeks to be worshiped as King. Even for Christians, culture is often king. But most of the things that are highly esteemed by our culture don't hold much value in the kingdom of God.

Our King isn't like any other king on the face of the earth. In the same way, the treasures of His kingdom aren't the same as the treasures we find in this life. The Bible makes some clear distinctions between treasures that are perishable and those that are eternal. Knowing the difference between the two and making the choice to pursue what lasts can be tough.

So much about our culture seems so alluring. It's difficult to believe that it is not as great as it seems. Even more dangerous is the lie that we *deserve* certain things: success, happiness, and money. Ultimately, those things don't satisfy.

If these things don't last, what's the point? What should be the focus of your life? The Bible gives us clear direction about the kind of treasure we should seek as daughters of the King. What's more, if we look closely, our culture gives us plenty of warnings about the consequences of pursuing things that don't ultimately matter.

What's the message?

Celebrities often define our lives. What they wear, we wear. What they buy, we buy. What they value, we often value. Pop culture is constantly sending us messages about what is valuable and worthy of pursuit. Because those messages are often embedded in movies, television shows, and song lyrics, sometimes we don't even recognize that a message has been sent. You and I must think critically about the values of this present world and the messages we are receiving.

To get your minds moving in that direction, I'm sending you on a scavenger hunt. Use your knowledge of pop culture and an Internet search engine to fill in the top 10 lists on the next page. Take the time to answer the questions that accompany each list.

Top 10 TV shows

1.	6.
2.	7.
3.	8.
4.	9.
5.	10.

■ What do these shows have in common?

■ What does this list reveal about what most Americans look for when making an entertainment choice?

■ List the underlying messages sent by these shows.

Top 10 songs

1.	6.
2.	7.
3.	8.
4.	9.
5.	10.

■ What subjects are addressed in the lyrics of these songs?

■ What messages do these songs send about what is valuable?

■ What do these songs communicate about what we think we deserve? (example: romantic love)

Top 10 goals of high school students
(Use your own thoughts and experiences for this list.)

1.	6.
2.	7.
3.	8.
4.	9.
5.	10.

■ Who has the greatest influence on high school students as they are setting goals for themselves?

■ How does the above list match up with your goals for yourself?

■ Based on this list, what do most students feel like they deserve?

King Solomon: culture creator

If you were making a list of the biggest stars 3,000 years ago, King Solomon would top the list. He was the third king of Israel and was chosen to rule by his father, David. The Bible says that Solomon was the wisest man who ever lived. He had it all—intellect, power, wealth, and popularity. He also can teach us much about the value of these "treasures."

Solomon sampled everything that he thought would give his life meaning. He probably felt like he deserved all the riches, pleasure, and fame he could acquire since he was the king. In Ecclesiastes 2:10, he wrote: *"All that my eyes desired, I did not deny them. I did not refuse myself any pleasure, for I took pleasure in all my struggles. This was my reward for all my struggles."*

Solomon tried everything he thought might bring fulfillment. Based on what you know about our culture, in what kinds of things would Solomon seek to find pleasure and meaning if He were alive today?

If we look at the Book of Ecclesiastes, we find that the cultural messages about what was important in Solomon's day weren't very different from the messages being sent by our own culture today. Solomon spent most of his life chasing after the same things that our culture tells us to pursue. The result? He found it all to be meaningless.

In Ecclesiastes 1:2, Solomon wrote his conclusion. Write it in the space below.

What does the word *futile or futility* mean?

If something is futile, that means it lacks value or significance. It is meaningless. When we apply this word to the messages of culture, we find that so much of what the world has to offer us and tells us to pursue has no real value.

Modern-day Solomons

Can you think of some modern-day Solomons? You can recognize them because they have everything that our culture values, including beauty, fame, wealth, and power, but their lives are a mess.

Look through some popular magazines and find out some information about a pop culture icon. Use the information you find to fill in the chart below.

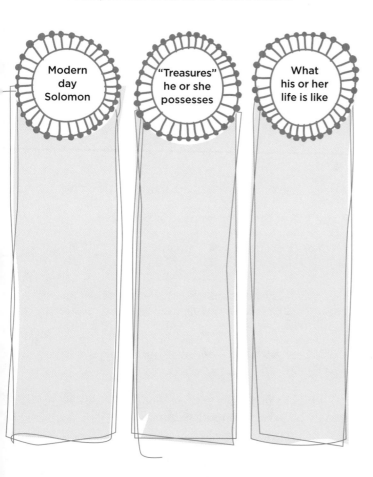

Modern day Solomon

"Treasures" he or she possesses

What his or her life is like

At first glance, Solomon's words in the Book of Ecclesiastes may seem pretty discouraging. Everywhere he looked for fulfillment, it slipped through his fingers and turned up empty. We find the same to be true by looking at the lives of many celebrities. Fame, money, power, achievement, and popularity aren't the treasures they appear to be.

The kingdom of this world is fleeting, but we serve the ruler of a Kingdom that will last. We don't deserve it, but we are the recipients of a Kingdom full of treasures that truly matter.

Read Matthew 6:19-21. What do these verses warn?

Spend some time praying that God would help you to recognize treasures that will last. Write out your prayer below.

Second Look

PART 1: Perishable vs. imperishable crowns

What do all of these things have in common?

- stainless steel
- aluminum
- diamonds
- uncooked pasta
- salt
- plastic

The answer? They are all things that won't spoil. Stainless steel and aluminum are metals that don't rust. Diamonds stay buried underground for thousands of years, but they never disintegrate. Salt and uncooked pasta have an almost endless shelf life. We've all heard that plastic lasts forever in our landfills.

Read 1 Peter 1:18-25. What does Peter say is perishable? What does he list as imperishable?

Go back to 1 Peter 1:24-25. Fill in the blanks below.

■ " For, All .... is like .... ,
and all its glory like .... The
grass .... , and the flower .... ,
but the .... of the Lord .... forever."

■ What did the writer mean when he described all flesh
like grass and its glory like the flowers of the field? ....
....
....
....

■ What will last forever? ....
....

What's the point?

The Bible doesn't say that material possessions are
inherently bad. It's OK to take good care of yourself and to
look nice on the outside. Money isn't evil. It's OK to want
to be liked by friends and to strive to achieve success in
school and work. The Bible isn't warning us to steer clear
of these things all together, but these passages do warn us
that beauty, wealth, popularity, and achievement won't last
forever.

The world promises that these things will make us
happy, but ultimately they don't hold their value. When
we get too wrapped up in the pursuit of these things,
our lives get out of whack. This is easy to recognize in
celebrities, but it usually sneaks up on us in our own lives.

**Give advice to these four friends who have lost
perspective on what matters. Write out your advice
beneath each scenario.**

*"I just don't feel pretty. Every other girl at school is thinner and
prettier than I am. No one ever pays attention to the way that I
look, and it is starting to bother me. There are some days that
it feels like my weight is all I think about. I don't have an eating
disorder or anything, but I've started skipping a meal or two here
and there to try and drop a few pounds. I would just feel so much
better about myself if I were beautiful." —Meghan, age 16*

....
....
....
....

"I'm graduating from college this year with a major in finance. It's not that I particularly love to study finance or that I'm even very passionate about it, but I want a career where I can make good money. My parents are both teachers, and I've watched them struggle from paycheck to paycheck my whole life. I don't want that for my family. It's not that I'm materialistic; I just want to be comfortable and not have to worry about money all the time." —Jessica, age 21

"I was just nominated to be on the homecoming court! Can you believe it? This is what I've hoped for and dreamed of for the past three years. It feels good to finally have some confirmation that people at this school like me. I really hope they choose me to be the queen." —Emily, age 17

"It's been my dream to be valedictorian since I was in first grade. I really want to be the number one student in my class, but it's hard work getting to that point. I have to have all As. Even one B in one class can disqualify me. If I get anything less than an A on assignments or tests, I totally stress out. Everyone knows that my goal is to be valedictorian. Even my teachers and counselors treat me like I've already achieved my goal. I certainly don't want to disappoint them. Sure, it's made my high school experience extra stressful, but I figure why not push myself to be the best. Right?" —Bethany, age 16

Did any of those stories sound like your own? Is it possible that you are too wrapped up in something that is destined to fade away? The point is not to avoid *everything* that won't last. That's impossible! But our best efforts should be focused on building what's eternal.

An imperishable crown

Paul addressed this very truth in 1 Corinthians 9:24-27.

If you could sum up this passage in one sentence, what would it be?

Paul's point was to run the race that matters. The analogy he used perfectly illustrates this truth. Think of Olympic athletes. They dedicate their entire lives to becoming the best at their sport. A select few of them manage to win gold medals, but to what end, ultimately? Their fame fades. Despite strict training, their bodies age. Eventually gold medals tarnish. There's nothing wrong with being an Olympic athlete, but Paul reminds us that ultimately, things of this world just don't last.

How long will the crown that Jesus has given us last?

Name three other things that are guaranteed to last forever.
- ■
- ■
- ■

Race toward what lasts

We serve an eternal King. He has promised us a Kingdom that will never end. Knowing that should change the way we live out our lives as daughters of our King. It will take some work, but our goal should be to pursue those things that hold eternal value and to spend less and less time in the pursuit of perishable crowns.

One way I can pursue the things that last is to...

Second Look

PART 2: Treasures

In bedtime stories, fairy tale princesses always have the very best stuff. Their dresses are gorgeous. Their castles are huge. Their carriages are fancy. When it comes to stuff, we expect princesses to have it all.

Materialism doesn't stay within the pages of fairy tales. The fascination with stuff is tightly woven into the fabric of our culture. Billions of marketing dollars are spent every year to convince you that money matters and possessions are the key to happiness. Without even realizing it, many of us adopt a materialistic mind-set and an approach to wealth that doesn't match up with the truth found in God's Word.

Since we are redefining royalty, let's take a look at what Scripture says about materialism and how we should approach money as daughters of the King. The Bible doesn't call us to avoid money and material possessions all together, but it does give us some principles to define how we can best approach our finances and possessions.

Money is . . .

Read the following verses and select the best summary for each.

Ecclesiastes 5:19:
- Money and possessions are gifts from God.
- Money and possessions come from being happy with my work.
- Money and possessions are the keys to a happy life.

Luke 12:15:
- Anyone who has a lot of material possessions must be greedy.
- My value to God isn't determined by money or possessions.
- If I have lots of money or possessions, others may see me as greedy.

Hebrews 13:5:
- It is wrong to love any possession.
- God has promised to provide for all of my financial needs.
- No matter how much is in my bank account, I can be content because God has promised He will always be with me.

Matthew 6:24:
- As a Christian, I shouldn't let money control the decisions I make.
- It's impossible to be a Christian and be rich.
- God asks me to hate money and material possessions.

1 John 3:17-18:
- I should use the money and possessions that God has given to me to minister to others.
- God asks me to give everything I have to the poor.
- Giving more means I love God more.

Based on what you've read, list three Biblical principles for handling money and possessions.
- ....
- ....
- ....

Are you materialistic?

1. You've had a terrible day. You failed your algebra test, missed every goal in practice, and got into a huge fight with your mom. You:
a) Pop in your favorite movie and lie around all evening.
b) Splurge on a double-dip ice cream cone.
c) Go to the mall to cheer yourself up by buying make-up and shoes you don't need.

2. Which of the following best describes your ride?
a) A 1990 used station wagon. First it was my parents', then my sister's, and now it's mine.
b) A fairly new SUV. My parents made the down payment, and I work to make a monthly car payment.
c) A brand new convertible. My parents bought it for my 16th birthday after I told them nothing else would do.

3. It's your birthday, and your grandma sends you a card saying that instead of a gift, she made a donation to a charity in your honor. You:
a) Get online and learn everything you can about the charity mentioned in the card. You're so impressed that you ask your grandma to donate to that same charity instead of giving you a Christmas gift.
b) Send a nice thank-you note but secretly wish for a present next year.
c) Call and thank grandma and drop a hint that in the future you'd prefer cash.

4. How many pairs of shoes do you own?
a) 5-10 pairs   b) 10-20 pairs   c) I've lost count

5. You're parents have asked you to get a summer job. You apply:
a) Anywhere that's hiring.
b) At all your favorite stores within 10 miles of your house so you won't have to spend most of your earnings on gas money.
c) Only at stores that sell cute clothes and offer an employee discount.

6. What's your opinion on labels?
a) Labels shmables.
b) You shop for bargains, but for jeans, you've got to have designer brands. They last longer, don't they?
c) Brands matter. You only shop at certain stores, and you want others to know it.

7. **Give yourself one point for each of the following items that you have. If you have more than one, give yourself one point for each. (For example, if you have three iPods˙, you would get three points)**

...... TV in your room   ...... iPod˙   ...... iTouch˙
...... Desktop computer   ...... Laptop   ...... Car
...... Video game system   ...... Cell phone   ...... Guitar
...... DVD player   ...... Designer purse (Coach, Louis Vuitton, etc.)

Give yourself 1 point for every A answer, 2 points for every B, and 3 points for every C. Then add up the points from question 7. Add point values from questions 1 through 7 to get your total score. Total score: ....

6-13 points. You're satisfied without stuff. You're fiercely practical. You'd rather find a bargain than buy name brands. You appreciate what you have and don't spend much time thinking about what you don't have.

14-22 points. Money's important to you, but it doesn't define you. You like to have nice things. You love to shop and like to receive expensive gifts, but you've got a practical side too. You've been known to have a diva moment from time to time, but you can live without most stuff.

23 points or more. Material girl alert! You need a big walk-in closet to contain all your goods. Stuff makes you happy, and you've got to have the best of everything. Others may see you as high maintenance, but you see yourself as a fashionista!

The heart of the matter

Jesus often taught about money. He didn't teach us to avoid money and possessions, but He did warn against allowing wealth and belongings to have a stronghold on our hearts.

Read Matthew 6:19-21 and answer the following questions.

■ What does Jesus warn us will eventually happen to the treasures we acquire here on earth? ....
....

■ What does He promise us about treasures we store up in heaven? ....
....

■ Jesus said that our treasures ultimately reveal what's in our ....

Read Matthew 6:24 and answer the following questions:

■ What's the difference between having money and allowing it to master you? ....
....
....

■ How can we know if we are serving money and material possessions more than God? ....
....
....

■ Are there any material possessions that occupy more of your time, thoughts, and energy than your relationship with God? ....
....
....

Go back to Matthew 6:21. Use that passage to fill in the blanks.

■ Where my .... is, my .... will be also.

Materialism isn't about stuff. Ultimately, what you spend your money on is really a reflection of what's going on in your heart. If you are storing up stuff, it's important to realize that those things are destined to fade.

What are some ways you can use the money and possessions that God has given you now (and in the future) to store up treasures in heaven? Write your ideas on the heart.

Second Look

PART 3: Do you deserve it?

Several years ago, I was doing research for a Christian book targeted at young women. I traveled the country interviewing Christian teenagers. As I interviewed over 100 young women, the phrase " I deserve" popped up over and over. These were *Christian* girls—leaders in their churches and youth groups. They told me that they knew in their heads that they didn't **deserve** certain possessions or achievements, but they admitted that their actions demonstrated a belief that they were *entitled* to certain things. You can read their actual statements[1] below.

In the sidebar, record your reaction to these statements:

> *"I deserve to get into a good college because of my studying and a really good relationship with my family."*

> *"I feel like I deserve whatever I work hard for because you just feel like that is balancing out."*

> *"...I deserve to have stuff before my sister. I deserve to have a cell phone before my sister. But no, when I got a cell phone, my sister got a cell phone. I deserve to have an iPod® and I deserve to have my own songs, but no, I have to download my songs onto my sister's iPod®."*

Many girls told me that they deserved certain achievements or possessions. Even more of them felt like they deserved for God to fix their problems. In fact, 62 percent of the girls admitted that they behaved like God should fix their problems and make their lives smooth. Many of us live like we believe we deserve certain things. We want God to respond the way we want, when we want it and to make us happy. It's time to ditch that diva mentality!

The genie prayer

If fairy tales are true, then a genie is just what every girl needs. Just rub a lantern, make a wish, and *poof*! You get what you want. The problem is that most of us see God as our own personal genie. In fact, many teens who pray regularly admit that the bulk of their prayer time is spent asking God for something.

List the things you have prayed about in the past 24 hours. Put each prayer into the following categories to see what types of prayers you pray the most. Write next to each item "Petitions" (asking God for things), "Praise/ thanks," "Confession," or "Listening to God."

■ ....

■ ....

■ ....

■ ....

■ ....

■ ....

A dose of truth

Read James 1:17 and Luke 11:11-13 and write them in your own words in the margin to the right.

■ What do these verses reveal about God? ....

....

Read 1 Peter 5:7. Write it out in the right margin.

■ What does this verse teach us about how God feels about our petitions? ....

....

Combine James 1:17, Luke 11:11-13, and 1 Peter 5:7 into a single summary statement. ....

....

Please hear this: **God cares about our circumstances.** He is a Father who wants to give good things to His children (Matt. 7:11). But He is more concerned with your *holiness* than your *happiness.*

Making the distinction

To be holy means to be set apart, pure, or sacred. We pursue holiness by making choices that help us be more like Christ. Holiness almost always requires sacrifice. Over and over, Jesus made hard choices in order to please the Father. He gave up an existence in heaven to come to earth for you and me. And He chose to go to the cross.

Jesus deserved comfort. But He didn't have an attitude of entitlement. He chose to live humbly and accepted a punishment He didn't deserve. He calls us to do the same.

Read 1 Peter 1:16 then fill in the blanks below.

■ For it is written, "Be ...., because I am ...."

This passage doesn't say, "Be comfortable because I am comfortable" or "Be happy." It tells us to seek holiness because of Christ's example. Does your lifestyle show that you are more concerned with being holy or being happy?

Next to each area below, write why you think you live like you're more concerned with *holiness* or *happiness*.

■ The way I treat my family..
■ The way I spend my time..
■ The way I spend my money...
■ My plans for the future...
■ My dating relationships...
■ The way I use my possessions...
■ My prayer life..

Thinking about thoughts

Our thoughts about what really matters shouldn't look like the world's. We need to shift our thinking away from the values of our culture and toward the things of God. Philippians 4:8 gives some clear guidelines for what to fix your thoughts on as you seek to pursue the things that will last.

Read Philippians 4:8 to fill in the blanks below.

Finally, brothers, whatever is ...., whatever is ...., whatever is ...., whatever is ...., whatever is ...., whatever is ....—if anything is .... or ....—think about such things." (NIV)

■ What thoughts in your life are unholy?...............................
....
....

■ What can you do to take those thoughts captive and make them obedient to Christ?......................................
....

■ I will spend less time pursuing the perishable stuff like
........................., ..., and ....

■ I will spend more time pursing the imperishable stuff like
........................., ..., and ....

Summing it all up

Here's a quick summary of what you've learned this week.

1. The things our culture .... **won't last. But
God's** .... **will stand** ....

In Ecclesiastes 1:2, Solomon described the things
our culture <u>treasures,</u> including beauty, fame, wealth,
achievement, and possessions, as futile. In Ecclesiastes
12:13, he reached the conclusion that the things that
culture promises will bring us fulfillment are destined to
fade away. We should seek the treasures that have value
in God's <u>kingdom</u> because it will stand <u>forever</u>.

2. God promises me an .... **crown.**

Material possessions and achievements won't last. They
are destined to spoil or fade away, but God's kingdom
will stand forever. Put your efforts toward things that
will hold <u>eternal</u> value in God's kingdom.

3. Where my .... **is, my** .... **will be also.**

God doesn't ask you to avoid money altogether but
to think about money with a Kingdom mind-set.
Ultimately, the way you spend your money and handle
your "<u>treasure</u>" is a reflection of what's in your <u>heart</u>.

4. God is more concerned about my ....
than my ....

God wants you to be like Him in His <u>holiness</u>. He doesn't,
however, exist to ensure your <u>happiness</u>. God is more
concerned about making you more like His Son than
making sure you are comfortable. The way we think

*"Absolute
futility," says
the Teacher.
"Absolute futil-
ity. Everything
is futile."
—Ecc. 1:2*

*"Now all has
been heard;
here is the con-
clusion of the
matter: Fear
God and keep
his command-
ments, for this
is the whole
duty of man."
—Ecc. 12:13
(NIV)*

*For where
your treasure
is, there your
heart will be
also.
—Matt. 6:21*

about God will impact our spiritual lives. The Bible encourages us to take every thought captive and make it obedient to God's standards.

Action step

Start or maintain the practice of tithing.
God is the giver of all things, including your financial resources. Throughout the Bible, He commands His followers to give back a portion of our resources to the church. This is a great way to begin spending your money in a way that reflects the biblical principles you've learned. You don't have to make big bucks do to it. You can give back a portion of the money you earn from baby-sitting, your allowance, or part-time job.

But don't stop with your finances. Giving back a portion of what God has given you is a principle that can be applied to all areas of your life. Here are some other ways to tithe:

1. **Tithe your time.** How can you use a portion of your time every day to minister to others?
2. **Tithe the possessions you already own.** Can you give up 10 percent of your clothes and shoes to someone who needs them? Can you dedicate 10 percent of the space in your room to God? (Try setting up a prayer corner or covering a portion of your walls with Scripture.) Think about ways to use your car to honor God and serve others.
3. **Devote a portion of your day to prayer.** How would it strengthen your faith to spend a percentage of each day in prayer and Bible study? God has given you 24 hours each day. How can you give a portion of your time back to Him?

Reflections of truth

Each week, you will write out one truth you learned this week, then place that truth on a mirror you use regularly. Write your weekly truth on an index card or sticky note or by using a dry erase marker directly on the mirror. Leave your truths up until the completion of the study and watch how it changes what you see in the mirror.

Week 4 Truth:
I will pursue the things that last!
1 Corinthians 9:24-27

ROYAL RESPONSIBILITY

Living as the King's Ambassador

First Glance

Way to go! You've made it two-thirds of the way through this study. Along the way, you may have discovered that taking off the tiara isn't always easy. Before we move on, let's take a quick check-up of how you're feeling about what you've learned.

Below is a list of 10 truths you've already learned and a couple of options for how you might be feeling. For each truth, circle the statement that reflects how you feel most of the time.

1. There is a big difference between acting like a princess and living like a daughter of the King.

   | I'd rather have the fairy tale. | OR | I'm excited about how the Bible defines my royal role. |

2. As God's adopted daughter, I have a responsibility to honor God and reflect His good name.

   | I am worried I'll mess up. | OR | I am a confident ambassador. |

3. My life is under the authority of the King. I am called to live a life in submission to Christ.

   | I am content to submit. | OR | I like to be in control. |

4. God is the One on the throne. I am a worshiper of God, not the one being worshiped.

   | I like being the center of attention. | OR | I love to attract others to Jesus. |

5. God is the only One worthy to be the most important thing in my life.

| I am making Christ #1 in my life. | OR | I am holding onto idols. |

6. God asks me to serve others by putting their needs ahead of my own.

| I am not sure how to serve. | OR | I am already plugged into a ministry. |

7. Living out my faith requires sacrifice.

| I'd rather be comfortable. | OR | I am willing to sacrifice. |

8. The treasures of this world are ultimately meaningless.

| I am afraid to be different. | OR | I am happy to go against the culture. |

9. God has promised me an imperishable crown.

| I am focused on life right now. | OR | I am willing to wait for my eternal reward. |

10. God is more concerned with my holiness than my happiness.

| I'd rather be happy. | OR | I'd rather be holy. |

These are some hard truths! Embracing them means making the choice to live for others in an all-about-me world. It isn't always an easy choice. Are you overwhelmed? Excited? Is your crown a little tarnished? Is your vision of princesses slightly shaken? Stick with me. In this session we'll look at the unique promises given to us as daughters of the King. We'll also discover some practical advice in God's Word for how to live as daughters of the King.

Letting go of the fairy tale

There's a lot to love about the lives of fairy tale princesses. They are the center of attention. Their lives look easy. Their closets are full of glamorous stuff. But there is a reality we must face about those princesses—they aren't real.

Who is your favorite fairy tale princess?

What is it about her life that is most appealing to you?

What excites you about the biblical description of a daughter of the King?

Read Titus 3:1-8. Write out the passage in the margin to the left. Identify three gifts God has given us. Circle them in the verses.

Gift #1

"He .... us—not by works of righteousness that we had done, but according to His mercy" (v. 5a).

■ According to verse 3, what did God save us from?

■ Sum up the items on this list in one word:

■ What is the ultimate consequence for that?

God saved us from the death that would inevitably accompany our sin problem. Now that's a rescue story! Don't you love it when a prince swoops in to save the princess in distress? That's the part of fairy tales that makes our hearts swoon. This passage reminds us that our own story isn't missing a rescue. God has swooped in, saved the day, and rescued us from sin and death.

Reflect on your rescue story. What was your life like before you accepted Jesus as your Savior? How has His forgiveness changed your life?

gift #2

"He saved us . . . through the washing of regeneration and .... by the Holy Spirit" (v. 5b).

■ What does it mean to be renewed?

■ What areas of your life has Christ changed to make them new?

■ In what areas of your life do you still need God to work to make things new?

God alone can take our messed up lives, broken hearts, and strained relationships and make them brand-new. In fairy tale terms, He finds us when we are paupers and makes us into princesses. Our lives are real examples of the rags-to-riches stories we love to read about in fairy tales.

gift #3

"So that having been justified by His grace, we may become .... with the hope of eternal life" (v. 7).

■ What does it mean to be God's heir?

■ What is our inheritance as heirs of God?

God adopted you into His family. As His adopted daughter, you will receive an inheritance of eternal life. This is another part of fairy tales that God makes real. Your father is the King. You are heirs to all that His kingdom contains. Right now you have the hope of eternal life with Him, and someday you will receive your inheritance.

Read 1 Peter 1:3-5. How does this passage describe our inheritance?

Compare the inheritance God promises us with the things we might inherit here on earth by drawing them in the boxes below.

Inheritance from God   Inheritance on earth

What God has given us is far better than anything we find in fairy tales. He has rescued us and made us new. He adopted us into His family and promises us an inheritance that can never be taken away. No sweeter story has ever been written. Then how should we live?

What our lives should look like

The Bible provides a lot of guidance on how to live as daughters of the King. The passage you just read in Titus is a great place to start because it gives us practical advice for what our lives should look like.

Go back and review Titus 3:1-8. Then give yourself a grade for how you are doing in each of the areas listed below.

- .... Being submissive to rulers and authorities
- .... Being obedient
- .... Being ready for every good work
- .... Not slandering (lying about) anyone
- .... Avoiding fighting
- .... Being kind/considerate
- .... Showing gentleness to all people
- .... Devoting yourself to good works

If you're looking for ways to live out your role as God's daughter, this list is a great place to start. Go back and circle one area you are going to work on this week.

PART 1: BE A LIGHT

Based on what you see and read in the news, how would you describe the world we live in? ....
....

We live in a fallen world. Wars rage across the globe. Leaders rise and fall from power. Natural disasters strike at random. Millions of people are hungry and hurting. But living in such a chaotic world isn't unique to your generation.

Look up the following passages and match them with the most appropriate word or phrase.

John 7:6-7	Evil
John 16:8	Dark
John 16:33	Sinful
1 Corinthians 7:31b	Temporary
Galatians 3:22	A place of suffering
Ephesians 6:12	Prisoner of sin/under sin's power

Because of sin, we live in dark world. Jesus, our King, brought a message of hope through His life and death on the cross. But until He returns, suffering will continue. How should this reality impact the way that you live?

Be a light in the darkness

Jesus didn't ignore the pain and suffering in the world around Him. Instead, He was a bearer of hope. In John 8:12 He said, *"I am the light of the world. Anyone who follows Me will never walk in darkness, but will have the light of life."* Jesus came to bring light to the darkness of this world. He asks us to respond to the world around us in the same way—by being a hope-bringer and light-bearer for the hurting and helpless and those lost in the dark.

Read Matthew 5:14-16, then answer the true/false statements on the next page.

READ ALL ABOUT IT! Gather 10 headlines from this week's news that feature ways our world is fallen. You can use newspapers, the TV, or an online news source. Write the headlines below.

1.

2.

3.

4.

5.

6.

7.

8.

9.

10.

T or F: Jesus describes me as the light of the world.
T or F: I should hide the light I've been given.
T or F: My light has the power to spread like the light from a candle on a stand.
T or F: I cannot control whether my light shines or is hidden.
T or F: One way to bring light to a dark world is through good works.
T or F: I should shine to draw attention to myself.

Based on what you know about light, use the chart below to compare the properties of light with how we should live as Christians.

Properties of Light:	How I should live:
It shows people a path	*Show people the way to God*

Living with compassion

Jesus is our greatest example for how to live as light in a dark world. He recognized that the people around Him were needy and hurting. He knew that their world was dark. And He responded to those people with compassion.

Define *compassion*.

Write down three examples from Scripture where Jesus responded with compassion.

■
■
■

Jesus called Himself the light of the world and asked us to live as children of the light. In the same way, He modeled compassion and then asked us to show compassion.

Read the following verses. Beside each, describe a situation in which you can respond like Scripture commands.

■ Ephesians 4:32

■ Colossians 3:12-13 ....

....

■ 1 Peter 3:8 ....

....

Living counterculturally

Another way to let your light shine is to live countercul-turally. In Matthew 5:14-16, Jesus told us not to hide the light He has given us. In other words, stop trying to blend in. Instead, we are to live in a way that is different than the world around us. The Bible is full of instructions for how to live differently than popular culture. For example:

• The world teaches that sex is a normal part of romantic relationships. The Bible teaches that sex should be saved for marriage (Heb. 13:4).

• The world teaches that skin is in. The Bible teaches that we should dress modestly (1 Tim. 2:9).

• The world teaches that it's all about you. The Bible teaches that it's all about Jesus (Col. 1:16-18).

• The world teaches that material things bring happiness. The Bible teaches that God alone can satisfy (Isa. 55:2).

• The world teaches that rules are made to be broken. The Bible teaches us to submit to authorities (Rom. 13:1).

• The world teaches that money is yours to spend the way you'd like. The Bible teaches that everything you have comes from God (Ecc. 5:19) and that you should use your possessions to serve God and others (Acts 4:32).

Think of two other ways that God specifically asks us to live differently than the world around us. Fill in the blanks below with your answers. Find a verse that supports each example.

■ The world teaches ....
  The Bible teaches ....
  Scripture reference: ....

■ The world teaches ....
  The Bible teaches ....
  Scripture reference: ....

Choosing to live according to God's Word instead of popular culture isn't easy. But God asks us to let our light

What scares you about living counter-culturally?

What excites you about it?

In what areas of your life are you already living counter-culturally?

Where do you need to make changes so your life looks less like the world and more like Christ?

shine in the darkness in order to point others toward Him. What's more, the standards He asks us to live by are designed with our best interests in mind. It may not always seem like it, but living by God's Truth, even when it's countercultural, truly is a better way to live.

Second Look

PART 2: Be a servant

Go back and review part 2—"How did He live?"— from session 3 on pages 52-54.

■ What has God already taught you about service through this study? ....
....

■ What steps have you taken to serve others? ....
....
....

■ What obstacles have you encountered to living a life of service? ....
....

In Luke 22:24-26 Jesus taught His disciples about service. What did He teach? Record your answers below.

■ Those who serve are .... in the kingdom of God.
■ Being a servant makes me stand out from the world around me because ....

This conversation took place soon after Jesus washed the disciples' feet. He had just modeled service to them as they sat down to eat. Their feet were probably still damp, and what were they doing? Arguing about who was the greatest! Instead of out-serving each other, they were duking it out to be number one. Things aren't very different today. Our culture still tells us to value being most important.

Choosing to serve others is still countercultural. Living a life of service to others isn't easy. It is difficult to put the needs of others ahead of our own—especially in a world that teaches, "It's all about me." Even so, Jesus calls us to follow His example.

Think of a time when someone else put your needs first and modeled Christlike service toward you. Use the prompts provided to write about that experience.

■ .... put my needs ahead of his/her own when he/she
....

■ Being served in this way made me feel ....
....

■ This experience taught me something new about God because ....
....

What about a time when you showed Christlike service to others? Write about that experience below.

■ I put ....'s needs ahead of my own by
....

■ I chose to serve him/her/them because ....
....

■ This act of service made me feel ....
....

Whom did Jesus serve?

Look up the Scriptures below and on the next page. Under each reference, write down whom Jesus served, how He served, and the result.

Matthew 8:1-3
■ Whom did Jesus serve? ....
....

■ How did He serve? ....
....

■ What was the result? ....
....

Matthew 14:13-21
■ Whom did Jesus serve? ....
....

■ How did He serve? ....
....

■ What was the result? ....
....

Matthew 20:29-34
- Whom did Jesus serve?
- How did He serve?

- What was the result?

John 4:3-30
- Whom did Jesus serve?
- How did He serve?

- What was the result?

What do these stories have in common?

Were the people Jesus healed seen as important in their society? Explain your answer.

What evidence can you find in these stories that Jesus served others even when it was inconvenient?

As I mentioned in session 3, it may be easier to serve some people than others. We tend to serve people we like or those who can return the favor someday. We like to serve when it's convenient. You may be willing to put others' needs ahead of your own when your schedule allows it or when your own life is running smoothly, but you may not want to serve when you are stressed and overscheduled. It's important to realize that Jesus didn't allow these barriers to stop Him. He served total strangers. Many were undesirable by society's standards. Jesus washed the disciples' feet when He knew His death was near. Talk about stress! No one would have blamed Him if He used that time for Himself. Instead, He chose to serve.

Jesus also taught us an important lesson: no task is beneath a servant. He taught and fed the 5,000 when He would rather have been alone. He spent time with the woman at the well even when it didn't fit His travel plans. He washed the disciples' feet even though it was a dirty job. In other words, He didn't see any act of service as being beneath Him.

Look at the list of service activities in the chart on the next page. Honestly assess which of the things on the list you'd be willing to do and which ones you would not by placing a check mark in one of the two categories.

WILLING | NOT WILLING |
☐ ☐ Volunteer in your church nursery
☐ ☐ Clean out gutters for an elderly woman
☐ ☐ Offer free baby-sitting to a single mom
☐ ☐ Share Christ with students at your school
☐ ☐ Groom (clip fingernails, brush hair and teeth, etc.) residents in a nursing home
☐ ☐ Clean toilets at a homeless shelter
☐ ☐ Pray with AIDS patients at a hospital
☐ ☐ Drive your siblings to and from school
☐ ☐ Work behind the scenes to plan worship services, even if no one acknowledges your work
☐ ☐ Serve as a long-term foreign missionary
☐ ☐ Give up your favorite activity in order to free up time to serve others
☐ ☐ Do more housework in order to serve your family
☐ ☐ Spend time with unpopular kids at your school even when others make fun of you for it

Are you willing to serve even when it involves sacrifice? Use the following prompts to help you think about this.

■ What do I see as beneath me?

■ Whom will I not serve?

■ When do I find it inconvenient to serve?

Spend some time praying for God to help you serve without barriers. Ask Him to reveal to you any person or act of service that you see as beneath you. Ask Him to give you the strength to serve like He did. Ask Him to lead you toward people who need to be served in the coming days and weeks.

Second Look

PART 3: Be an ambassador

 Are you an ambassador?

1. A friend at school asks why you're wearing a Christian T-shirt. You:
a) say, "It was clean, so I thought I'd wear it."
b) explain that your youth pastor encourages you to wear Christian T-shirts to school.
c) use the opportunity to share your faith.

2. Your pastor announces that he needs volunteers to join a street evangelism team. You:
a) doodle on your church bulletin and pretend you didn't hear him
b) sign up for another ministry to avoid being asked to join the evangelism team
c) sign up and start preaching

3. Talking about your faith makes you feel . . .
a) scared to death
b) anxious you will say the wrong thing
c) excited

4. When your youth group goes on mission trips, you:
a) don't go
b) sign up for service teams and let others do the evangelism
c) look forward to the opportunity to share your faith

5. In order to share the gospel with others, you need . . .
a) a lot of Bible knowledge
b) a great testimony
c) a willing heart

6. How many times have you shared the gospel in the past six months?
a) none   b) a few times   c) lots of times

7. Telling others about Jesus is . . .
a) not my spiritual gift
b) something I do out of obligation
c) something I am passionate about

8. Telling others about Jesus is . . .
   a) the job of pastors and evangelists
   b) for Christians who have the gift of evangelism
   c) something God calls all Christians to do

How did you do? The quiz was designed to help you start thinking about your attitude toward sharing the gospel with those who do not know Jesus. Even if you've been a Christian for a long time, sharing your faith can feel intimidating. In today's lesson, we'll look at how evangelism fits into your calling as a daughter of the King.

go and tell

Review Part 1 of Session 1 on pages 12-13. How did you define "ambassador" in the margin of page 13?

According to what you learned on pages 12-13, what responsibilities do you have as Christ's ambassador?

An ambassador is someone who represents the king in special events and meetings and who protects the good name of the king. This is a part of your role as a princess. But the Bible also asks you to be Christ's ambassador by sharing the gospel with non-Christians.

This command is most clearly seen in Matthew 28:18-20 when Jesus gave the Great Commission. Write out that passage in the margin.

■ Just before Jesus ascended into heaven, He gave His disciples a to-do list. In the verses you just wrote, circle the three actions Jesus asked His disciples to take.

■ Summarize each of these action steps in a single word.
   1. _____ 2. _____ 3. _____

Jesus was essentially telling His disciples to **go** and share the Truth of the gospel, to **lead** people to Christ, and to **disciple** people. He commissioned these 11 disciples to be ambassadors of the gospel. The New Testament tells the story of how these men boldly shared the gospel with the hurting world around them. As a result of their efforts, many came to know about the love of God, and the good news of Jesus spread worldwide.

Christ gave the Great Commission to His disciples more than 2,000 years ago, but that command still applies to Christians today. We have been adopted into God's kingdom and understand that the world around us is dark. We have a responsibility to tell others how they can come out of the darkness and into the light of God's family.

Write out the following Scriptures in your own words. Beneath each one, list the principle in that verse that will help you be Christ's ambassador.

■ Acts 20:24

■ Romans 1:16

■ 1 Corinthians 9:16

■ Galatians 1:10

Sharing the good news of Christ is an important part of living out your royal responsibility. The Bible encourages us not to be ashamed of the gospel and to boldly tell others about God's grace.

What obstacles keep you from sharing the gospel with others?

What steps can you take to overcome those obstacles?

What motivation do you have to fulfill the Great Commission?

Write down the names of three people who need to know about God's grace. Think about it in stark terms: *Whom do you not want to go to heaven without?* **Commit to pray for their salvation regularly and ask God to give you opportunities to share the gospel with them. When God provides that opportunity, take it!**

1.   2.   3.

Summing it all up

Here's a quick summary of what you've learned this week.

1. As a daughter of the King, I have been given unique gifts. Titus 3:1-8 reminds me that I have been ...., ..., and made Christ's ....

Titus 3:1-2 tells us how to live as daughters of the King. Titus 3:3-8 reminds us of why we should live this way. Jesus has <u>saved</u> us, <u>renewed</u> us, and made us <u>heir</u>s to His kingdom. He has given us so many gifts and promised us a future that is better than any fairy tale.

2. God calls me to be a .... in a .... world.

According to Matthew 5:14-16, we are to be the <u>light</u> in a <u>dark</u> world! God gives us the awesome responsibility of piercing that darkness with the hope that can be found by knowing Jesus. You can be a light for Jesus by treating others with compassion and living counterculturally.

3. God calls me to .... others by putting their .... ahead of ....

As Luke 22:26 states, the rules are different in God's kingdom! We don't get to be the star based on popularity or by being the best at sports or academics. Jesus urges us to work hardest at serving others. He saw no one as unworthy of being served, and no act of service was beneath Him. As His daughter, you need to seek to <u>serve</u> others even when it's inconvenient by putting others' <u>needs</u> ahead of <u>your own</u>.

4. God has commissioned me to be an .... of the ....

We are the adopted daughters of the King. He has given us the awesome responsibility of sharing the hope that we've found in Him with others. (See Rom. 1:16.) Being <u>ambassador</u>s of the <u>gospel</u> of Jesus is an important part of living out our royal role.

"Let your light shine before men, so that they may see your good works and give glory to your Father in heaven." —Matt. 5:16

"But it must not be like that among you. On the contrary, who-ever is great-est among you must become like the youngest, and whoever leads, like the one serving." —Luke 22:26

For I am not ashamed of the gospel, because it is God's power for salvation to everyone who believes. —Rom. 1:16a

Action step

Get some training on how to share your faith with others. Your church or youth group might already offer a class on sharing your faith. If this is the case, sign up to take the class at the next opportunity. If no class is available, make an appointment to talk with your pastor or another leader about how to share the gospel with others. Ask him or her to give you some basic tips about how to talk to others, as well as some Scripture references you can study for more information.

Reflections of truth

Each week, you will write out one truth you learned this week, then place that truth on a mirror you use regularly. Write your weekly truth on an index card or sticky note or by using a dry erase marker directly on the mirror. Leave your truths up until the completion of the study and watch how it changes what you see in the mirror.

> **Week 5 Truth:**
> **I am an ambassador of the gospel!**
> Matthew 28:18-20

Then Jesus came near and said to them, "All authority has been given to Me in heaven and on earth. Go, therefore, and make disciples of all nations, baptizing them in the name of the Father and of the Son and of the Holy Spirit, teaching them to observe everything I have commanded you. And remember, I am with you always, to the end of the age." —Matt. 28:18-20

NOTE: Your next group study will look very different than in previous weeks. Your group leader will lead you in two activities designed to help you reflect on what you've learned during the course of this study and think through how you will live differently as a result.

I would encourage you to come to this final session prepared for God to do a work in your heart. He still has much to teach you about who He is and what it means to be adopted into His family. In your life, there are probably still areas of selfishness that need to be surrendered to Him and changes that need to be made in order to live out your royal role.

Come prepared to worship the King. Come ready to serve Him by serving others. Come willing to lay yourself down at His throne.

CASTING YOUR CROWNS

First Glance

Today's study will look very different than previous ones. First, you will participate in a worship service designed to draw you to the throne room of God. Then you will continue to worship the King by serving together. This will allow you to start living out your redefined role as a princess.

God still has much to teach you about who He is and what it means to be adopted into His family. Are you ready to worship the King and serve Him by serving others? Are you willing to lay your life down at His throne?

Return to the throne room

Let's go back to the vision of our King we first saw in session 2. Revelation 4:1-11 describes a powerful image of our King on His throne. To begin the worship service, you will meditate on this image of Christ using an ancient practice called *Lectio Divina*, which literally means "divine reading." It is a way to intentionally focus and pray through God's Word. You can use it to focus on any passage of Scripture.

Getting started

Move to a place in the room where you are not distracted by others. Get comfortable and begin the time by spending a few minutes in prayer or by simply sitting quietly. Once you are focused, open your Bible to Revelation 4:1-11 and move through the four phases of *Lectio Divina* listed below.

Phase one – *Lectio*: Reading
What does the text say? Read the passage slowly several times. Don't try to absorb the whole passage at once. Just like you don't eat a whole meal in one bite, don't try to take in the whole passage quickly. Read slowly enough to savor each portion of the Scripture. Pay attention to any words or phrases that jump out at you.

Phase two – *Meditatio*: Meditation
What does the passage say specifically to me? Reflect on the image of God portrayed in this passage.

Specifically think about how this Scripture applies to your own life. Get personal. Think about where you are in your life right now and how the love of the King you've just read about should make a direct impact on how you live.

Phase three – *Oratio*: Prayer
What does God say to me, and what do I want to say to Him? Talk to God about what you've just read. Tell Him what stands out to you about this passage and what you've realized about yourself. You may need to thank Him or praise Him. You may need to confess sin.

Phase four – *Contemplatio*: Contemplation
What is God saying to me? Be still and silent in the presence of God. Allow Him to speak to your heart about what you've read and how He wants you to apply it.

Laying it down

Draw two contrasting pictures below. In the picture frame on the right, draw an image of what the world says it means to be a princess. In the picture frame on the left, draw an image of the 24 elders as described in Revelation 4:10-11.

Around that throne were 24 thrones, and on the thrones sat 24 elders dressed in white clothes, with gold crowns on their heads.
—Rev. 4:4

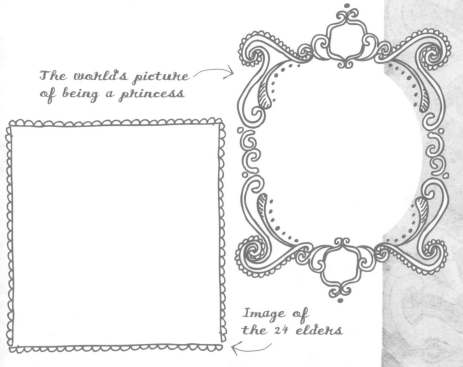

The world's picture of being a princess →

Image of the 24 elders ←

*The 24 elders
fall down
before the
One seated
on the throne,
worship the
One who lives
forever and
ever, cast their
crowns before
the throne, and
say: "Our Lord
and God, You
are worthy to
receive glory
and honor
and power,
because You
have created
all things, and
because of
Your will they
exist and were
created.
—Rev. 4:10-11*

The elders were obviously important people. In Revelation 4:4, we read that they each had a throne of their own. They were dressed in fancy robes and crowned with golden crowns.

In a world that teaches us to focus on ourselves, it's hard to comprehend how these elders behaved. They had been given many of the gifts our society values—power, prominence, and favor. Verses 10 and 11 tell us what these elders did with those gifts and in doing so, gives us a powerful image of surrender. They didn't keep their crowns. They didn't use their crowns or their thrones for their own glory. Instead, they laid their crowns at the throne of Jesus and acknowledged that He was the only One worthy to be glorified.

You have been given gifts as well. The tiara you are wearing is symbolic of all the things God has given you. He has adopted you as His daughter. He has made you an heir to His kingdom. He has given you treasures on earth, such as talents, abilities, and relationships. You can use those gifts to draw attention to yourself, or you can lay them at the foot of God's throne.

You will be spending the next several minutes worshiping God through music, prayer, and art. When you're ready, lay your tiara down before the cross. This is symbolic of laying yourself down before the King of kings!

Time to reflect

Laying my life down at the throne of God means
....
....
....

I want to lay my life down because
....
....
....

One part of my life I find difficult to lay down at God's throne is
....
....
....

PART 1:
Remember the crowns you've been given

I'll never forget the first moment I saw it. I was in a bridal shop having my wedding dress fitted. I wasn't looking for a tiara, but when the sales clerk pulled one out from a display case and placed it on my head, I felt like I'd just been crowned Miss America. It was the most beautiful tiara I had ever seen. I had to have it. On my wedding day, it was my favorite thing I wore. The crown I wore on my wedding day was beautiful. It will always be something I treasure. But at the end of the day, it's just metal and rhinestones. It won't last forever. It can't give me anything more than a precious memory.

Most crowns are like that.

Throughout this study you've learned that the treasures of this world are bound to tarnish. The "crowns" that the world promises will bring you glory are destined to rust. Society's definition of royalty is based on things that inevitably fade.

That's easy to remember when you're involved in this Bible study, but living out God's definition of royalty really begins when this study ends. He hasn't challenged you to live as His daughter for only six weeks. These truths are designed to change how you live for the rest of your life.

A man who endures trials is blessed, because when he passes the test he will receive the crown of life that God has promised to those who love Him. —Jas. 1:12

The crown of life

Read James 1:12. God has given me the crown of ....

Look up the following verses. Record the kind of life each Scripture promises.

■ John 3:16 ....

■ John 10:10 ....

■ Romans 6:4 ....

■ Ephesians 5:1-2 ....

God is able to give us a life we could never earn for ourselves. Most importantly, God offers us eternal life through Jesus. Because of Christ's sacrifice, we will spend forever (can you even grasp how long that is?!) in heaven with Him. This gift alone is better than anything the world has to offer. But He doesn't stop there! God offers us new life as believers. He also came to provide a way for us to experience His love and abundance here on Earth. What a wonderful crown!

The crown of righteousness

Read 2 Timothy 4:8. God has given me the crown of

....

There is reserved for me in the future the crown of righteousness, which the Lord, the righteous Judge, will give me on that day, and not only to me, but to all those who have loved His appearing.
—2 Tim. 4:8

Which of the following correctly define *righteousness*? Circle all that apply.

Justified

Perfect

Freedom from guilt or sin

Blameless

Made right

Immoral

Condemned

Proud of yourself

Righteousness means freedom from guilt or sin. Because God is holy, we must be righteous in order to be in His presence. But there's a problem. Romans 3:10 tells us "There is no one righteous, not even one." Because of our sinful nature, we cannot achieve righteousness on our own. That causes separation between us and God. But as you just read in 2 Timothy 4:8, God promises us a crown of righteousness. Through Jesus' death on the cross, He provided a way for us to be free of sin and guilt.

You could never have earned the crown of righteousness on your own. You can't be good enough or pretty enough or popular enough to free yourself from your own sin. But God has given you the crown of righteousness because of His great love for you.

What else has God given you that you could never have earned on your own? Make a list below....................................

....
....
....
....
....
....

The crown of glory

Read 1 Peter 5:4. God has given me the crown of

....

We give glory to the things we think are important. What does the world glorify? ....

....

Write about a time when others glorified/praised you for something you did. ....

....

How did that make you feel? ....

....

How long did the glory last? ....

....

And when the chief Shepherd appears, you will receive the unfading crown of glory.
—1 Pet. 5:4

The world gives us glory based on what we *do*. Being the best means getting the earthly glory. We glorify movie stars and professional athletes, scholars and heroes. The problem is, most of us will never make it to Hollywood. Most of us will be weekend athletes. Most of us will never have the chance to be scholars or heroes. Even if we are, we won't stay that way forever. Lasting glory is yet another thing we cannot earn for ourselves. But God promises to crown us with a kind of glory that will never fade away.

Laying down your crowns

The crowns that God gives us are spectacular! They are better than anything the world has to offer. This is an important thing to remember when we are tempted to pursue the glory that gives us temporary fulfillment instead of the imperishable crowns that will last forever.

Every day, you make choices to either pursue a temporary crown or to pursue the kind of crowns you can lay at the feet of the One who has adopted you as His daughter. It's not a choice you make just once. Being a princess means constantly laying your crowns down at God's throne.

Write God a letter (below or in your journal) thanking Him for the crowns He's given you. Tell Him that you want to lay them back at His feet so that *He* can be glorified. Ask Him to help you live out His vision of royalty.

Second Look

PART 2: Surrendering your selfishness

The world tells you it's all about you. God's Word teaches that it's all about Him. These two truths are polar opposites. Your life will look totally different depending on which truth you choose to embrace.

In order to live like a daughter of the King, you must surrender your selfishness. Just like the laying down of your crowns, this isn't the type of surrender that happens once. Living out your Christian faith means constantly surrendering your will to God. It will take effort to keep your focus on Jesus rather than on yourself.

The scoop on selfishness

Selfishness means being excessively or exclusively concerned with oneself. In other words, it is living a life that is me-focused rather than God-focused or others-focused. We may not like to think that we are selfish, but the truth is we often consider our own needs first. This leaves no room for a life that is focused on glorifying Christ.

Here are some examples of how the message of selfishness appears in mainstream marketing. Match the advertising slogan with the correct brand below.

Because you're worth it™   Burger King

Obey your thirst™   McDonald's

Have it your way™   Visa

It's everywhere you want to be™   L'Oréal

I'm loving it™   Sprite

Living as if your own needs and desires are the only things that matter is contradictory to God's Word. As Christians, God asks us to surrender ourselves to His will and put the needs of others ahead of our own.

The following Scriptures focus on the truth about self-ishness. Beside each passage, write down the principle for surrendering selfishness.

■ Psalm 119:35-37

■ Galatians 5:19-21

■ Philippians 2:3

■ James 3:16-17

■ Romans 2:6-8

In summary

Here's a quick summary of what you might have written beside those Scriptures above.

1. Turn your heart toward God's .... and away from .... gain.

In Psalm 119:35-37, the writer asked God to turn His focus toward God's <u>will</u> and away from <u>selfish</u> gain. If you have a hard time accepting the truth found in God's Word because it requires sacrifice or keeps you from living the life you want for yourself, that's evidence that you've bought into the selfishness encouraged by the world. Repeat the prayer found in Psalm 119:35-37. Ask God to turn your heart away from your selfishness and toward His Word.

2. Pursuing .... ambition is an act of my .... nature.

In Galatians 5:19-21, the writer Paul listed <u>selfish</u> ambition among the acts of the <u>sinful</u> nature. Living as if you are all that matters isn't just selfish, it's sinful. Recognize that selfishness is a big deal to God.

3. Consider _____ **better than** _____ .

Philippians 2:3 urges us to do nothing out of selfish ambition but to humbly consider <u>others</u> better than <u>ourselves</u>. Make a conscious effort to consider the needs of the people around you and take advantage of every opportunity to put their needs ahead of yours.

4. _____ **leads to** _____ .

You learned in James 3:16-17 that <u>selfishness</u> goes hand in hand with <u>disorder</u>. Living like you are the only one who matters isn't God's plan for your life. And honestly, focusing too much on yourself will only lead to chaos. In fact, being selfish often leads to conflict with others. The second part of this verse reminds us that it is wise to be considerate of others. If you have been inconsiderate and selfish to someone you know, apologize for your selfishness. Ask them how you can better meet their needs in the future.

5. Those who are _____ - _____ **will receive God's** _____ **and** _____ .

Romans 2:6-8 teaches believers that those who are <u>self</u>-<u>seeking</u> will receive God's <u>wrath</u> and <u>anger</u>. Evaluate your own life for selfish attitudes and behaviors. Confess your selfishness to God. Ask His forgiveness. Ask Him to change your heart.

Your selfishness score

Do you live like it's all about you? Or do your choices show that your focus is on Jesus? Evaluate how you live in each of these areas using the following scale.

1 – It's all about me
2 – I still have some work to do
3 – I'm not sure
4 – I am focused on others
5 – It's all about Jesus

_____ The way I spend my time
_____ The way I treat my family
_____ The TV shows I watch
_____ The way I spend my money
_____ My plans for the future
_____ The way I treat people no one likes
_____ What I think about most often
_____ My involvement in my local church

_____ The way I dress
_____ Who I am online
_____ The way I talk
_____ The music I listen to
_____ My attitude toward sin

In which areas of your life is it most difficult for you to focus on the needs of others? Explain.

Write down any areas where you gave yourself a 1, 2, or 3 in the list above. Next to each area, write down one action step you can take to shift your focus away from yourself and toward Jesus.

Surrender your selfishness

On each of the points of the crown below write down an area of selfishness you are willing to surrender. Then find a specific Scripture that encourages you to make a change in the area you listed. Because surrendering your selfishness is not a one-time event, take some time this week to recreate your crown and place it somewhere prominent (such as in your Bible, journal, or on your bedroom door) as a reminder of your commitment and God's truth.

"Remember this: the person who sows sparingly will also reap sparingly, and the person who sows generously will also reap generously. Each person should do as he has decided in his heart—not out of regret or out of necessity, for God loves a cheerful giver."
—2 Cor. 9:6-7

PART 3:
Becoming a princess who perseveres

Let's fast-forward about six weeks. You've committed to start living like a daughter of the King. You're working to practice humility, sacrifice, and service on a daily basis. You've been doing pretty well so far. A few people have even told you that they see a difference in you.

Then the worst day ever comes along.

You oversleep, leaving no room for Bible study or prayer. Your siblings are annoyed because you've been driving them to school lately and now you're all going to be late. Your mom's in a bad mood and cuts you zero slack. When you start to show a little attitude, she throws all the work you've been doing back in your face. "I see the princess is back," she says. *Argh!*

Things don't improve at school. Your friends are too busy to notice you're stressed. No one helps you with anything even though you've been going out of your way to meet the needs of others the past few weeks.

When you get home, you just want to be alone. But your sister wants to play a game, your dad wants you to help him clean the garage, and your mom wants you to set the table.

How would you feel?

What would you say or do?

What Scriptures from this study come to mind when you think about the scenario above? Write them down.

On days like this, you realize that embracing humility in an all-about-me world isn't easy and doesn't always pay off the way that you would like. Not everyone will recognize your service or sacrifice. Some people will take advantage of you. You'll miss out on some things. Living out God's

vision of a princess will take some work. You'll need to develop perseverance and persistence.

God does not promise that living according to His plan will be easy. In fact, He frequently warns us through His Word that tough times will come. But God promises a prize to those who persevere.

The following Scriptures will help you develop a plan to become a princess who perseveres. Fill in the chart to see that plan take shape.

	Action Step(s)	Prize Promised
1 Corinthians 9:24-27		
Galatians 6:7-10		
Ephesians 6:10-20		
Philippians 3:12-14		
2 Timothy 2:1-13		

God's Word gives us the tools we need to live the life He calls us to live. He gives us reminders of the gifts He has promised. If we will focus on His promises, they can motivate us when it seems easier to live for ourselves.

What are some other action steps you can take to help you live out what you've learned? List them below. I've given you a few examples to get you started.

- Ask one of the girls from your Bible study to be your accountability partner. Meet regularly to talk about how you are doing at living out what you've learned.
- Make a regular service commitment. Ask to be put on the rotating schedule for working in your church nursery, make a weekly commitment to serve at a soup kitchen, or volunteer at a local crisis pregnancy center.

Add your ideas here:
- ....
  ....

■ ....
....
....
■ ....
....

A different kind of prince

Change is hard. Making changes to the way we think and live in order to be more like Christ is really, really hard. To help you live like a daughter of the King, I want to take a look at some of the obstacles you are likely to face. We've spent a lot of time looking at the King of kings in this study. But before we conclude, there is a prince who should be mentioned.

Daniel 10:13 describes him as the prince of Persia.
Matthew 12:24 calls him the prince of demons.
John 16:11 says he is the prince of this world.

Who are these verses describing? If you guessed Satan, you're right. Satan isn't the heir to God's throne. He is not a part of God's royal family. But he does have some authority to rule over our current world. The Bible warns us that he seeks to distract us from God's plan for our lives.

Look up the following verses. What does each one tell us about Satan? Write down your answers.

■ 1 Peter 5:8 ....
....

■ John 8:44 ....
....

■ John 10:10 ....
....

Satan is a destroyer, a liar, and a thief. First Peter 5:8 warns us to be alert to His attacks. However, we don't need to be afraid of him. First John 4:4 promises us that the One who is in us (Jesus) is greater than the one who is in the world (Satan). But it is wise to be aware that you may face some opposition as you seek to live your life according to God's Word.

What are some ways you can protect yourself against Satan's attacks? Find a verse or phrase that supports each action step and write it down, too.

■ ....
....

■ ....
....

■ ....
....

■ ....
....
....

■ ....
....

Be a persevering princess

Summarize the following verses below.

■ Hebrews 10:35-36 ....
....
....

■ James 1:2-3 ....
....
....

■ James 1:12 ....
....
....

What do all of these verses encourage you to do? ....
....

Which of the words or phrases below correctly define the word "persevere"? Circle all that apply.

Be determined	Carry on	Give up
Endure	Go for it	Quit
Surrender	Keep going	Press on
Stay the course	Hesitate	Stick with it

Choose from the list of circled words to fill in the blanks below. You can use words more than once.

■ When it is easier to focus on myself instead of others, I will ....

■ When service feels inconvenient, I will ....

■ When I forget who's really on the throne, I will ....

■ When the world around me tells me to value comfort more than sacrifice, I will ....

■ When I want others to worship me instead of the King of kings, I will ....

■ When I am tempted to live like earthly treasures will make me happy, I will ....

There will be days when humility, service, and sacrifice will be tough. On those days, remember the crowns that you have already been given and the prizes God promises to the people of His kingdom.

Summing it all up

Here's a quick summary of what you've learned this week.

1. I will .... the crowns God has given me.

In a world that teaches us to focus on ourselves, it is hard to imagine <u>laying</u> <u>down</u> our lives before God. But that is exactly what He asks us to do because He is the only One worthy of glory and honor and praise.

2. God has given me the crown of .... , the crown of .... , and the crown of ....

First Corinthians 9:25 says, *"Now everyone who competes exercises self-control in everything. However, they do it to receive a perishable crown, but we an imperishable one."*

The crowns that God gives us are spectacular! They are better than anything the world has to offer. This is an important reminder when we are tempted to pursue the glory that gives us temporary fulfillment instead of the imperishable crowns that will last forever—crowns of life, crowns of glory, and crowns of righteousness.

3. Being a princess means surrendering my ....

Philippians 2:3 says, *"Do nothing out of rivalry or conceit, but in humility consider others as more important than yourselves."*
God calls us to shift our focus away from ourselves and to focus on serving Him and others. Surrendering your selfishness isn't easy in a world that teaches us to look out for number one.

4. When temptations come, I will be a princess who ....

James 1:12 says, *"A man who endures trials is blessed, because when he passes the test he will receive the crown of life that God has promised to those who love Him."*

Living out your faith won't always be easy. Satan will tempt you to revert to living like it's all about you. Trials will come that will make serving others feel impossible. God's Word urges us to keep moving toward the prize, even under these circumstances.

Action step

Take everything you've learned and pass it on. Make a commitment to mentor a young woman who needs to hear God's Truth. Here are some ideas for how to get started.

- Talk to your children's pastor about leading a princess party for the younger girls in your church. Make plans to pamper them (think tea party or spa night) while finding ways to teach them what you've learned about what it *really* means to be a princess.

- Do this study with a younger sister or a younger girl from your youth group. Do the big group studies together and meet regularly to discuss what she's learning through the individual study.

Now everyone who competes exercises self-control in everything. However, they do it to receive a perishable crown, but we an imperishable one.
—1 Cor. 9:25

"Do nothing out of rivalry or conceit, but in humility consider others as more important than yourselves."
—Phil. 2:3

A man who endures trials is blessed, because when he passes the test he will receive the crown of life that God has promised to those who love Him."
—Jas. 1:12

- Create a mentor program with the other girls from your study. Ask an adult in your church to help match you up with a younger girl who needs a mentor and then work together to teach the principles you've learned in this study.

- Start a blog. Write frequent posts about what it means to live like a daughter of the King and how you're living out these principles in your daily life. Talk to other girls you know and ask them to read your blog and comment on it. Also ask them to post their own stories of how they are embracing humility in an all-about-me world.

Reflections of truth

Each week, you have been asked to write out one truth you learned, then place that truth on a mirror. Write out your last weekly truth on an index card or sticky note or by using a dry erase marker on the mirror itself. Continue to leave your truths up on display after you've finished this study to see how it continues to change what you see in the mirror.

> **Week 6 Truth:**
> **I will continue to lay my crowns
> down at God's throne.**
> Revelation 4:10-11

"The 24 elders fall down before the One seated on the throne, worship the One who lives forever and ever, cast their crowns before the throne, and say: 'Our Lord and God, You are worthy to receive glory and honor and power, because You have created all things, and because of Your will they exist and were created.'"
—Rev. 4:10-11

Leader Helps

A word from Erin

I am thrilled that you have decided to teach God's Word to the young women in your community. Because we live in a culture that teaches us to focus on ourselves, there is a need to point women toward God's truth, which teaches them to say no to selfishness and yes to a life that is focused on loving God and serving others. You will explore that truth together throughout this study.

The foundation of this study is God's Word. He has already provided the most important lessons on what it means to live like a daughter of the King. As the group leader, saturate your own life with His truths. Prepare your heart to teach by reading His Word often and listening to what He has to say.

Prepare for this study through prayer. There is a lot to do in preparation to teach a Bible study like this. It can be easy to focus on your to-do list and forget to pray for God to move. Recruit some prayer partners to pray with you and for you while you teach. We have prayed for you as we've prepared this resource.

Adapt this study to best fit the needs of your group and learners. As you make changes to activities and schedules, consistently point your students back to God's Word, which will teach them how to live like true princesses. I celebrate with you as the girls in your study ditch the diva attitude and start to live like daughters of the King of kings!

Grace and Peace!
Erin Davis

SUPPLIES NEEDED:
- One copy of *True Princess* for each girl
- 5 large sheets of paper
- Markers and pens or pencils
- Computers or phones with Internet access or several Bible concordances
- Index cards for prayer prompts

OPTIONAL:
- One journal for each girl
- Copies of well-known children's books about princesses
- Video clips from several princess movies

OPENING OPTION #1
Set up your room to match the description given in the first paragraph of page 8. Create a tea party atmosphere with white linens, fine china, and beautiful centerpieces. Pamper the girls as they come in and provide a tiara for each girl to wear. Once

SESSION 1:
THE TRUTH ABOUT ROYALTY

Opening

Hang four (4) large sheets of paper around the room. Place several markers near each sheet. At the top of each sheet, write one of the headings from the list below.
- *Words connected to "princess"*
- *Favorite stories about princesses*
- *Scripture verses about princesses*
- *Images associated with princesses*

Direct girls to write their thoughts on the sheets of paper. They shouldn't spend too much time on any one area.

Take a closer look

Instruct girls to close their eyes. Read aloud the scene in the first paragraph of page 8 of the book. Then ask the girls to open their eyes and tell you where they think the scene you described is taking place.
SAY: This scene wasn't ripped from the pages of a magazine. This isn't a royal banquet inside a castle. In fact, this scene can be found often in church youth rooms. The girls made to feel like princesses are *you*. ASK: Where exactly does this idea that you are princesses come from? What exactly does it mean to be a daughter of the King?

Group activity

Divide girls into groups of two or three to complete the activity found in the margin of page 8. If Internet access is available, allow girls to use an online Bible search engine (*www.Biblegateway.com*) to search for the word "princess" in the Bible. If the Internet is not available, provide concordances for each group and ask them to find Scripture references for the word "princess."
SAY: You are the adopted daughters of God. Since He's the King of kings, that makes you a princess. But we'll also learn that our idea of what it means to be a princess doesn't always match up with God's vision for our lives.
Discuss what the girls have written on the large sheets of paper throughout the room. Ask girls why they wrote what they did. Direct girls to complete "Defining a princess" on page 8. Direct girls to copy their answers

from the questions at the end of that section onto a large sheet of paper.

ASK: Does our definition of princess match up with the way we are described in God's Word? Let's find out.

Proving your royal heritage

Instruct the girls to look up the four verses on page 9. Call on a girl to read 1 Timothy 6:15-16 out loud. Direct girls to write out the part of Scripture about royalty. Repeat this process with the remaining verses. **SAY: The point? God is the King! He has adopted you as his daughter. That makes you a princess!** (student book fill-in-the-blank).

Direct girls to write a note of thanks in their books or in journals you've provided to Jesus for adopting them.

SAY: There's a huge difference between acting like a princess and being the daughter of a king.

Ask girls the questions listed on page 10. They may struggle to answer some of these questions because they are so far removed from what we associate with princesses. That's OK. Let them struggle. Point out the fact that we rarely consider a princess' responsibility to her father. **SAY: You aren't just called to act like princesses. You are called to honor the King.**

Choose someone to read Psalm 45:11 out loud. **ASK: What does this passage say about how God feels about you? What does this verse say about how you should respond?** Give girls time to answer the questions on page 10 individually. Discuss how they plan to honor God.

Making the distinction

Direct girls to turn to the chart on page 11. Discuss the difference between being a princess and being a daughter of the King. Direct them to record their answers.

Alone time

You will wrap up your study each week by giving girls time alone. This time will help them process what they've learned and let God speak to them about their lives. The tone of the room should be quiet and reflective. Guide the time with the activities below.

Quiz: Which kind of princess are you?
Tell the girls to complete the quiz on page 11. It will get them thinking about how they live.

Prayer prompts
Place index cards throughout the room with specific prayer prompts written on them. Encourage girls to move silently from card to card using each prompt as a way to begin a conversation with God. They can record their thoughts/prayers in their journals. Use the list of prayer prompts on page 6 or supplement them with your own.

Journal
If you incorporate journaling into your large group time, conclude this session by asking the girls to journal about what they have learned and what God is teaching them.

SESSION 2:
WHO'S REALLY ON THE THRONE?

Opening

As the girls arrive, hand them each a stack of 5 to 10 index cards. Tell them to write on each card words or phrases that describe Jesus (one per card). Designate a place for them to display their cards once they are finished and to talk and mingle until everyone arrives.

SAY: Last week we learned that you are princesses. This week we will take a look at who is really on the throne. Before we dig in, let's review what you've learned so far in your individual study.

Summing it all up

Direct the girls to turn to the "Summing it all up" section on page 23. Quickly review the four main points from the session. Don't spend too much time on review; leave plenty of time for teaching new material.

POINT 1: God is the King. He adopted me into His family. That makes me a princess! (student book fill in the blank). ASK:
■ What is the difference between acting like a princess and living like a daughter of the King?
■ What is God teaching you about what it means to be His daughter?

SUPPLIES NEEDED:
• index cards (5-10 for each girl, plus some for prayer prompts)
• paper
• pens/pencils
• highlighters

Note: Spending some time reviewing the week's lessons will encourage participants to do their individual study, give them a chance to ask questions, and help to further cement the study's content in their hearts and minds.

POINT 2: "Everything I do brings glory or dishonor to God. In other words, I am Christ's <u>ambassador</u>." ASK:
- Have you been living as if your reputation is the only one at stake?
- What actions will you commit to take in order to better honor God? (Review their answers on page 13.)

POINT 3: In order to <u>follow</u> the rules of God's kingdom, I must regularly read His <u>Word</u>. ASK:
- What obstacles prevent you from reading the Bible regularly?
- What steps can you take this week to read the Bible more often?
- Have girls share the commitment they made on p. 18.

POINT 4: When I submit my life to Christ, I am in for a <u>God</u>-sized <u>adventure</u>. ASK:
- What did you learn about the benefits of submitting your life to God?
- What is one area where you need to submit to God?

Redefining kingship

Turn girls' attention to the descriptive terms they wrote on the index cards. Discuss the words. If anyone wrote the word "King," ask her to describe what kind of king Jesus is. If no one wrote the word "King," draw attention to that fact. Ask the girls why they don't necessarily think of a king when they think of Jesus.

SAY: **Our God is all of the things listed, but He is also our powerful King. He is the Ruler of the entire world and seeks to be the Ruler of our individual lives. When we see the throne room of God, there is no doubt who has the right to reign.**

What's your image of the King?

Tell the girls to complete the activity on page 26. They can either describe God's throne room in words or pictures. Read Revelation 4:1-11 out loud. **ASK: If you could describe the King in this passage in one word, what would it be?**

Group girls into pairs. Direct them to read Revelation 19:11-16 and complete the activities on page 27. Then bring the girls back together. Direct them to close their eyes as you read Revelation 4:1-11 and Revelation 19:11-16. Tell the students to open their eyes.

OPTION
Give girls some time to share what they learned by completing the action step on pages 24.

OPTION
Invite someone to come and share about how God taught her to shift the focus from herself. This might include:
1. An individual who was focused on a specific career path until God called them elsewhere.
2. Someone who was changed on a mission trip.
3. A mom who sacrificed her own needs in order to care for small children.
4. Someone who has endured hardships (illness or job loss) and learned how big and capable God is.

OPTION
Because this session focuses on worship, you could conclude with a time of corporate worship. If you have a worship team or worship leader available, ask them to lead your group in a time of worship. Choose songs that focus on God the King.

ASK: How is the King described? How would you feel if you were in the throne room? What would you say if you were face to face with this King? Where would you be in this throne room?

SAY: You are not the center of attention. You may be a daughter of the King, but these passages clearly show that God is on the throne. This perspective should lead you to a place of humility. Your focus should shift from an "all about me" mentality to the King.

Popcorn prayers

Tell the girls that the focus of this prayer time is to thank God for the kind of King that He is. Remind them that this is not a time to focus on their own needs, but to focus on the kind of King they serve. In no particular order, girls should pray using the following: *"Jesus, thank You for being a_____ King. Teach me how to focus on You."*

Alone time

Direct them to focus on their powerful King. Tell them to worship Him by writing a poem or song lyrics in His honor on the bottom of page 28. Give them a chance to share what they've written.

Prayer prompts

Place index cards throughout the room with specific prayer prompts written on them. Encourage girls to move silently from card to card using each prompt as a way to begin conversation with God. If they'd like, they can record their prayers in their journals. Use the prompts on page 6 and/or supplement them with your own.

Journal

If you incorporate journaling into your large group time, conclude this session by asking the girls to journal about what they have learned and what God is teaching them.

SESSION 3: ROYALTY REDEFINED

Opening:

Place the following items on a table in the front of the room. As girls arrive, allow them to play with and talk about the items until everyone arrives.

cell phone	answering machine	laptop
envelope	fax or fax machine	bouquet of flowers
note in a bottle		

ASK: What do these items have in common? Give the girls time to respond. **SAY: These are all ways to send a message. SAY: Did you ever play the telephone game when you were a kid? The original message almost always gets lost in transmission. Today we will learn what happened when our King had a message to send. But first, let's review what you learned last week.**

Summing it all up

Direct the girls to turn to "Summing it all up" on page 41. Review the four main points from the session. Don't spend too much time on review to avoid redundancy and leave plenty of time for teaching new material.

Point 1: God is my King. My role is to worship, not to be the one worshiped. ASK:
■ How did the passages in Revelation change your image of Him?
■ What are some ways that you try to get others to focus their attention on you or worship you?

Point 2: Whatever is most important to me will become my idol. ASK:
■ Based on what you learned, how would you define the word "idol"?
■ What are some idols you identified in your own life?

Point 3: When my circumstances are difficult, it's important to remember that I serve a good King. ASK:
■ If you don't believe God is good, how does that make an impact on how you live?
■ What challenges in your life make you feel like God isn't a good King?

Point 4: I can approach God's throne with boldness through prayer. ASK:
■ How do you feel knowing that you serve an approachable King?
■ How would you rate your prayer life this week?

Transition into this week's session by asking: **In movies and fairy tales, how do kings usually send a message to the citizens of their kingdom?**

SUPPLIES NEEDED:
• some or all of the items listed in the opening section
• pens or pencils
• markers
• several sheets of poster board or art paper (one per pair of girls)
• scissors
• glue
• magazines
• index cards for prayer prompts

ACTION STEP
For last week's action step, the girls were asked to recruit a prayer partner. Ask them to share who their prayer partner is. If they've not yet found one, help them think of girls who would make good partners or match up members of your group to be prayer partners.

121

SAY: We are accustomed to hearing royal messengers make announcements on behalf of the king. But Christ is no ordinary King. He doesn't match up with our image of royalty. He rarely does things the way other kings do. This is especially true when He has a message to send.

The message arrives

Direct girls to complete the activity on page 44. Give them an opportunity to read aloud what they wrote. **ASK: Who does "The Word" describe in this passage? SAY: Remember from the previous session that the Word of God is one of the names given to Jesus (Rev. 19:13). That same passage also describes Jesus as the King of kings. When we connect the dots, we see that John 1:14 is describing a truly unique event—Jesus, the King of kings, became a man and lived among His people! This truth becomes even more amazing as we examine the way our King arrived.**

Group girls into pairs and have them read Luke 2:1-20. Provide each group with a poster board and magazines they can use to create a collage of words that describe Jesus' birth. Ask groups to share their work. Then instruct girls to individually answer the questions on page 45.

What does the message mean?

SAY: Jesus came to earth to bring <u>good</u> news to <u>all</u> people. The good news is that He is our <u>Savior</u>. (student book fill in the blank) **ASK: But what did He come to save us from?** Direct girls to look up the four Scriptures on page 46 and write down the phrases that describe why our King came to save us. Give the girls time to share their proclamations of Christ's birth.

Alone time

Ask the girls to write out their testimonies as a way to reflect on God's role as their Savior. Tell them to focus on what their life was like before Christ, what their life is like with Christ, and what promises they have been given for the future because Jesus is their Savior. If any girls want to share their stories, allow time for them to do so.

Prayer prompts

Place index cards with specific prayer prompts written on them throughout the room. Encourage girls to move silently from card to card using each prompt as a way to begin a conversation with God. If they'd like, they can record their prayers in their journals. Use the list of prompts on page 6 and/or supplement them with your own.

Journal
If you incorporate journaling into your large group time, conclude this session by asking the girls to journal about what they have learned and what God is teaching them.

SESSION 4:
THIS PRESENT KINGDOM

Getting ready:

This week's group time will take extra preparation on your part. Make sure to allow enough time to gather and set up the needed items.

Foot washing ceremony

1. Place enough chairs for the students and leaders in a circle around a large banner or flat bedsheet.
2. Play soft music or leave the room silent. Your goal is to create an environment that allows the girls to focus fully on this activity.
3. Place a dish of washable paint near each chair.
4. As the leader, you will start the process by helping one of the girls dip her feet in the paint and then press them onto the banner.
5. Take a tub of soapy water and wash the paint off of the girl.
6. Each participant will dip her feet (or hands) in the paint and then place them on the large banner.
7. Then, girls will each take turns having their feet (or hands) washed by another member of the group and washing another's feet (or hands).
8. Instruct the students that while they are having their feet washed, they should not help with the washing process. You want them to experience what it is like to be served.

Make sure everyone takes a turn washing the feet (or hands) of others.

Once everyone has participated, move the girls into a time of individual contemplation by asking the discussion questions in the margin of page 124.

SUPPLIES NEEDED:
- flat bedsheet or sheet of paper large enough to create a banner
- washable paint
- paper plates or pie tins for paint
- tub(s) of soapy water and (old) towels
- soft music and speakers (optional)
- index cards
- tape
- magazines
- markers

Name that celebrity

On each girl's back, tape an index card containing the name of a celebrity. Choose celebrities who seem to have it all but whose lives are a mess. Do not let the girls see which name has been taped on them. They must ask yes or no questions to deduce the name taped to them.

When girls have identified the celebrities on their backs, collect the cards. You will come back to these names later in this session. **ASK: What does it mean to be a celebrity? Based on who's famous in our culture, what characteristics do we value as a society? What parts of celebrities' lives do you envy? What parts of their lives are you happy to live without? Is there evidence in these celebrities' lives of an "I deserve" mentality? Explain.**

What's the message?

SAY: Celebrities often define culture. What they wear, we wear. What they buy, we buy. What they value, we value. But, celebrities aren't the only barometers of culture.
Group girls into three teams and direct them to turn to page 63. Lead teams to develop a top 10 list using the Internet or their own knowledge. Assign each group to one of the top ten lists (TV shows, songs, goals). After several minutes, allow one member from each group to share their list with the large group. **ASK: Based on these lists, what does our culture value? What does our culture tell us we deserve? What messages does culture send you about what will make you happy? Do cultural messages match up with the messages from our King? Explain.**

King Solomon: culture creator

Read Ecclesiastes 1:2 to the group, then **ASK: What does the word *futile* (or *meaningless*) mean? How does this word apply to the messages of culture?**

Modern-day Solomons

Direct girls to the chart found on page 65. Assign to each girl a specific celebrity from the game you played earlier. Tell girls to fill in the chart, based on the celebrity they have. **SAY: At first glance, Solomon's words in Ecclesiastes may seem discouraging. Everywhere he looked for fulfillment turned up empty. We find the** same to be true for many celebrities. Fame, money, power, achievement, and popularity aren't the treasures they appear to be. So where should we look for fulfillment?

Direct a girl to read Ecclesiastes 12:13 to the group, then **ASK: According to this verse, how can we find fulfillment?** Invite the group to move back to the banner you created during the foot-washing activity. Read Matthew 6:19-21. **ASK: What does this verse promise? How should knowing that God's throne lasts forever influence the way we live?** As a group, write Matthew 6:19-21 on the banner.

Alone time

Instruct girls to spend time asking God to help them to recognize treasures that will last.

Prayer prompts
Place index cards throughout the room with specific prayer prompts written on them. Encourage girls to move silently from card to card using each prompt as a way to begin a conversation with God. They can record their thoughts and prayers in their journals. Use the prompts on page 6 and/or supplement them with your own.

Journal
If you incorporate journaling into your large group time, conclude this session by asking the girls to journal about what they have learned and what God is teaching them.

SESSION 5: ROYAL RESPONSIBILITY

Opening

Read the 10 statements on pages 80-81 of the study. Each statement gives two options for how the girls may be feeling at this point. Tell girls to move to one side of the room or the other based on how they feel about each statement.

SAY: Embracing these truths means making the choice to live for others in an all-about-me world. It isn't always an easy choice. In this session we will look at the unique promises given to us as daughters of the King.

ASK: What excites you about the kind of princess God wants? What truth seems the most difficult to live out? In what areas is God challenging you to make changes?

SUPPLIES NEEDED:
- Index cards for prayer prompts
- large sheet of paper and markers (optional)

Letting go of the fairy tale

ASK: Who is your favorite fairy tale princess? What is it about her life that is most appealing to you?
SAY: There is a reality we must face about those fairy tale princesses—they aren't real. God's Word teaches us how to live out our royal heritage.

Read Titus 3:1-8. Direct the girls to write out the verse in the margin of page 82. **SAY: This passage reminds us of three gifts God has given each of us. Go back and see if you can identify those three gifts. Circle your answers.**

Gift #1—"He <u>saved</u> us—not by works of righteousness that we had done, but according to His mercy" (v. 5a).
ASK: According to verse 3, what did God save us from?
SAY: God saved us from our own sin. More importantly, He saved us from the punishment for our sin—death. Now that's a rescue story!

Give the girls time to reflect on their own rescue stories. In their journals, tell girls to write about what their lives were like before they accepted Jesus as their Savior and how His forgiveness has changed their lives. Give them time to share what they wrote with the group.

Gift #2— He saved us through the washing of regeneration and <u>renewal</u> by the Holy Spirit" (v. 5b).
ASK: What does it mean to be renewed? The dictionary defines *renewed* as being "like new." What areas of your life has Christ made like new? What areas of your life does God still need to make like new?
SAY: God can take our messed up lives, broken hearts, and strained relationships and make them new. He finds us when we are paupers and makes us princesses.

Gift #3—"So that having been justified by His grace, we may become <u>heirs</u> with the hope of eternal life" (v. 7).
ASK: What does it mean to be God's heir? What is our inheritance? Direct a girl to read 1 Peter 1:3-5 aloud.
ASK: How does this passage describe our inheritance?

Alone time

Direct the girls to read the "What our lives should look like" section on page 84 and complete the activity during their time alone with God. Be available for anyone who wants to pray about changing a specific area of her life.

OPTION
Copy the activity from page 84 onto a large sheet of paper or chalkboard. Direct the girls to fill in the chart by comparing and contrasting the inheritance God promises us with the things we might inherit here on earth.

Prayer prompts

Place index cards throughout the room with specific prayer prompts written on them. Encourage girls to move silently from card to card using each prompt as a way to begin a conversation with God. If they'd like, they can record their prayers in their journals. Use the list of prompts on page 6 and/or supplement them with your own.

Journal

If you incorporate journaling into your large group time, conclude this session by asking the girls to journal about what they have learned and what God is teaching them.

SESSION 6: CASTING YOUR CROWNS

Getting ready

This week's group time will take extra preparation. Make sure to allow enough time to gather and set up the needed items. In this final session, you will provide two activities to help girls reflect on what they've learned and think through how they will live differently as a result.

First, you will lead the girls in a worship service that focuses their attention on God and gives them an opportunity to surrender their lives to Christ. Then, you will put what you've learned into action by completing a service project as a group. If time constraints prevent you from completing both activities in one session, do them separately. Both activities are equally important to help cement the content of the study in the hearts and minds of your girls.

Return to the throne room

As each girl arrives, put a tiara on her head. Play quiet worship music to create a contemplative atmosphere.
SAY: To begin our worship time, you will meditate on this image of Christ using an ancient practice called *Lectio Divina*. *Lectio Divina*, which means "divine reading." It is simply a way to focus and pray using God's Word.
Instruct girls to turn to page 98 of their books and read about the four phases of *Lectio Divina*. Once everyone has read the explanation, instruct girls to move to a portion of the room where they won't be distracted by others. Direct

NOTE TO LEADERS: Session 6 will look and feel very different from the previous sessions. For more specific instructions and ideas, check out the teaching plans on page 126. Be sure to read these plans several days before the last session as some prior planning is required.

SUPPLIES NEEDED:
- Tiara for each girl
- Worship leader or worship music and sound system
- Large sheet of paper
- Markers

**DISCUSSION
QUESTIONS:**

1. How has this passage changed your image of God?
2. How has this passage changed your image of yourself?
3. Has God revealed anything specific to you personally through this study? Explain your answer.
4. How will understanding God's role as King impact your life in the future? Be specific.

SERVICE ACTIVITIES:

1. Go to a nursing home and help groom residents (clip fingernails, wash hair etc.).
2. Reach out to a single mom. Babysit her child. While she is gone, clean the house and cook.
3. Volunteer to serve at a soup kitchen. Help clean up after the meal is served.

them to get comfortable and begin the time by spending a few minutes in prayer or by simply being quiet.

Say: Once you are focused, open your Bible to Revelation 4:1-11 and move through the four phases of *Lectio Divina* at your own pace.

After girls have completed the exercise, lead a discussion by asking the questions in the margin to the left.

Laying it down

Instruct the girls to complete the art activity on page 99. To keep the mood contemplative, play soft music and encourage the girls to work alone instead of talking.

SAY: The 24 elders were obviously important people. We read that they each had a throne of their own. They were dressed in fancy robes and crowned with golden crowns, but they didn't keep their crowns for themselves. They didn't use them for their own glory. Instead, they laid their crowns at the feet of Jesus and acknowledged that He was the only One worthy to be glorified. You have been given crowns as well. The tiara you are wearing is symbolic of all the things God has given you. You can use those gifts to draw attention to yourself, or you can lay them at the foot of God's throne.

Worship

Move into a time of worship. Bring in a worship leader who can lead the group in a time of collective worship. As an alternative, play a DVD of worship songs and images.

SAY: You will be spending the next several minutes worshiping God through music, prayer, and art. Focus your attention on Jesus. Use this time to sing to Him, write praises to Him on the large sheet of paper posted on the wall, or pray. When you're ready, lay your tiara down on the floor. This is symbolic of laying yourself down before the King of kings!

Go serve

Immediately following the worship service, lead your group in a service activity. Choose an activity (such as one in the margin to the left) that will push girls out of their comfort zones and encourage them to serve others in a way that isn't glamorous or convenient.